MICHAEL KRÜGER

DIDEROT'S CAT
Selected Poems

Translated by Richard Dove

GEORGE BRAZILLER

First published in the United States of America in
1994 by George Braziller, Inc.

English translation © by Richard Dove
Originally published in German

Copyright © 1993 by Residenz Verlag under the title
Diderots Katze

For information, write to the publisher:
George Braziller, Inc.
60 Madison Ave.
New York, NY 10010

Library of Congress Catalog Number: 93-73823

Printed in the United Kingdom
First U.S. Edition 1994

Contents

Acknowledgements

I would like to thank the Aschendorffsche Verlagsbuchhandlung for permission to translate an alternative version of 'Meister' – *Ernst Meister in memoriam* – which appeared in H. Arntzen/J.P. Wallmann (ed.), *Ernst Meister, Hommage*, 2nd edition, Münster, 1987; the editors of *Grand Street* (New York) and *proposition* (Tübingen) for allowing me to reproduce (in some cases reworked) versions of the *Diary-Poems*; those, especially Friedrich Frieden, Regina Fritsch and Jürgen Dziuk, who discussed points of detail with me; and, of course, Michael Krüger for our various conversations, by letter and in the flesh.

RD

Introduction

If the recent German *Zeitgeist* could speak, it might sound a good deal like Michael Krüger. Through a glass darkly, it is possible to make out the mood of the times from the uneasy summer preceding the terrorist-ridden 'German Autumn' of 1977 to the second 'German Autumn' of 1989 and beyond ('20th October 1989' is clearly, among other things, a reaction to Honecker's fall two days previously). His world is, recognizably, the peace-time world of the *Wirtschaftswunder* and of subsequent economic and cultural down- and upswings: the ringing of a telephone, which is about to rip apart a house, customs officials 'tearing apart' a car, a near car-crash are, outwardly, the most dramatic happenings. And, despite poems concerning Littlehampton, Sussex and Princeton, New Jersey, the Mediterranean and the Near East, and despite more than fourscore Roman elegies, there is none of the escapist exoticism to be found in so much contemporary verse. Krüger's characteristic landscapes and inscapes are specifically German – small spots like Haag in Upper Bavaria (p.98), the South East with its 'boards for the dead' (p.143), Berlin (where he was brought up) and Munich (where he lives). Gottfried Benn's arch-romantic 'Southern Word', blue, is conspicuous by its rarity.

This does not mean that he is a homely idyllicist: in the recent collection *Idyllen und Illusionen*, the 'illusions' far outnumber the (environmentally polluted) 'idylls' and the only place-name in the German-speaking world to be mentioned (Hitler's birthplace) testifies to the author's concern about the ever-present threat of fascism. Even when he appears to come close to reportage, as in 'My new apartment, Liebigstr. 7', his work remains far removed from undialectical verism – as the pensioners' flying wives make clear. Indeed, the closer one looks, the greater the impression of alienation, of distance. The first collection, not least on account of the massed references to spleens, ganglia, inflamed nerves and acedia, appears to constitute a disaffected anatomy of modern German melancholy; and an astringent avowal from the second – 'My feelings towards the natives are mixed:/I understand their lingo,/their customs are quite beyond me' (DK 16)[1] – betrays the typologizing gaze of the anthropologist. But it would perhaps be most fitting to think of Krüger as a kind of archaeologist of the present. In a period in which *Betroffenheit*, with its connotations of deep, if perhaps myopic, emotional involvement in burning issues, has been a buzz-word, the cold eye he has cast on contemporary life is that of someone searching – as it were – *post festum*. References to archaeology are not uncommon either. The praise lavished on the archaeologist's profession in one of the novellas seems, for once, quite devoid of irony: '...only patient boring and scooping around in the maternal earth will, once again, be able to give us some idea, some image, of

what we have lost, have frittered away, for good' (*Warum Peking?* p.16).
And it is, hardly accidentally, to an archaeological metaphor that Krüger
resorts to adumbrate his childhood:

> I am my parents'
> fourth child, born
> in Germany, in the last war.
> The dim, distant past or
> yesterday, now –
> the strata can no longer
> be distinguished,
> clearly, that is... (DK 15)

In other respects too, it is the author's distance from the trends of the
time which is striking. Admittedly, a number of early poems share the
preoccupation of *Neue Subjektivität*, a loose grouping in the ascendant in
the late 1970s, with 'the self' in a banal, post-optimistic milieu. But they
decline to purvey the customary unbuttoned confessionalism, 'With a
head full of booze and movies'.[2] One of the earliest poems expresses con-
tempt for 'sweating I-sayers' (R 22) and – as the recurrent image of the
mask intimates – there is, from the start, a decidedly poststructuralist
doubt about the integrity of 'identity'. There is also an unfashionable ten-
dency to rise and survey the contemporary scene from odic heights:
'Munich-Stuttgart and back' cunningly echoes Hölderlin's hymn 'Patmos'
(it can, and perhaps should, be read as the 'Patmos' of the Economic Mira-
cle) and the unpopular predilection for *Gedankenlyrik*, philosophical
poetry, was recognized early on. Similarly, although ecological concern is
in evidence in some of the first poems, the approach (unlike that of so
much *Ökolyrik*) is indirect – taking the form of whimsical fantasias (as in
'What Times are these', a riposte to a celebrated poem by Brecht) or of
fleeting aperçus (as in the *Diary-Poems*). By the same token, Krüger's scep-
ticism towards 'regular' verse did not diminish in the 1980s when the 'Re-
turn of Form' (Harald Hartung) had many West German poets striving
to breathe new life into the metres of Klopstock and Heine. With few
exceptions (the triumphant sand/hand, for instance, in 'A Letter from
Rome'), his rare rhymes sound either sarcastic or deliberately accidental;
his typical sonnet has always limped and had thirteen lines; in 'Archaeol-
ogy' the precious couplet-form painfully chafes the colloquial content
(and *vice versa*). And, even though one does come across 'perfect' iambic
pentameters and dactylic hexameters, they seem like decoys to deceive the
uncritical harmony-addict (Krüger has written in this connection of the
need to position metrical stumbling-blocks 'in order to irritate the ear'[3]).
    Similarities with modish *littérature citationelle* are similarly superficial.
When what is without doubt the Bocca della Verità in Rome is described
as 'ein Kunstgebild der echten Art,/das keiner achtet' ('true artefact, the
real thing,/that none respects') (D 7), the unhappy few might possibly be

flattered to recognize the reference to a major Mörike poem. The same may also hold true in the case of the lines from one of Hölderlin's obscurer odes, 'Der Zeitgeist', quoted in '19th Century' ('Dread all round...') or, say, in the case of the brief excerpt from Emerson's essay 'The Over-Soul' (p.93). But the sheer volume of fragmentary citations from the most heterogeneous sources is bound, in the end, to bewilder even the professed polymath. Krüger's 'allusive' style is, in reality, mock-allusive – a socratic, or sadistic, challenge to the reader's complacency, to his or her capacity for perception. It is for this reason that no notes have been appended to this selection: although foreign readers may, perhaps, benefit from knowing that Erich Arendt was a hermetic East German poet (p.49) and that Paul Wühr is an experimental Bavarian writer (p.50), Krüger is more concerned with the 'deep structure' of experience than with the kind of accidentals that are grist to the mill of crossword puzzles. It would be counterproductive, for instance, to guess at the identity of the paintings which lie behind the cycle *Lida's Pocket Museum*: the poems are indeed based on real paintings, but on ones which have frequently been telescoped to produce an imaginary painting.[4] And there is no way that one can – or should need to – know the name of the mansion in 'Guided Tour of a well-known house'.

The fact is that the pre-eminent theme of this apparent chronicler of his times is a timeless one – the problem of 'reading' the present correctly (DK 9), the problem of perception *per se*. It can be no coincidence that the relativizing concept of perspective, encountered repeatedly in his work, should be planted at the very start of the programmatic opening poem 'Dedication', nor that it should inform an attack (in the name of the many potentialities within everyone) on the social myth of 'continuous' identity in a retrospect on the first collection: 'But straightforwardness, that much-admired product of modern Reason, is a tight-fitting mask which compels our look, that keeps coming from the same, rigid, never-changing angle, to continue in the selfsame never-changing direction' (R 74). It is true that the title of the poem 'Anamorphosis' appears to suggest that there is a standpoint from which everything begins to fall into place – an anamorphosis being, after all, a distorted projection which, when viewed from a particular point, seems regular and 'properly' proportioned – but the poem in question appears only to compound confusion. As Gombrich has pointed out, there is no rigid distinction between perception and illusion.[5] But, when setting traps for the unwary reader, Krüger is clearly out to induce the latter 'to weed out harmful illusions'.[6] For, despite his various *trompe l'oeil* effects, phrases like 'the hoax of perspective' (D 39) imply an almost Platonic distaste for art's deceptive imitations. The carpenter in the *Republic*, when making a couch, is translating the idea of the couch into matter and is thus at only one remove from the idea itself whereas the artist who represents the carpenter's couch is copying the appearance of a single couch and is thus twice removed. Accordingly, a poem which

Krüger himself sees as central to his canon, *Kleines Seestück* (Minor Seascape), concerns someone sitting staring at the ocean through a 'half-blind' mirror, through the 'distorted' glass of the window, and thus unable to tell whether a fly is 'really' on the window, on the mirror, or somewhere out at sea (AdE 72ff).

As a result, for all the verisimilitude of the scenes from contemporary life, it is not merely socratic irony when the speaker in *Über eine Fliege* ('On a Fly') confesses: 'Reality is not my strong point' (D 13). Krüger's typical poem is, as it were, an omnium gatherum which excludes neither the humdrum here-and-now, daydreams, wisps of fairy-tales, gleanings from books nor the most outlandish of allegories. It is quite possible, as in a poem set in Greece in December 1978, for a Murderer of Dreams suddenly to emerge and stand all those assembled in a village café a round of drinks (AdE 96-97). Indeed, it is often as though the author were at pains to pass on his own categorical uncertainty about reality – or rather 'realities' (D 13) – to the reader in the form of 'picture puzzles intended to perplex the beholder'.[7] In a prose work, a would-be critic attempts to fuse the sentences of his subject (a nineteenth-century philosopher) with his own commentary in order to obtain a 'physiognomy in which three elements interlock to form a picture puzzle [*Vexierbild*]: the "face" of the century, the "face" of the philosopher and my own' (*Was tun?* p.25); and a reviewer was surely not wrong to draw attention to the affinity with the mannerist painter Arcimboldo.[8]

Even in the case of such apparently innocent pieces as *The fire-brigade's blue light keeps leaping*, one is inevitably sucked into a troubling hermeneutic circle. Is one faced with no more than a little Roman cameo? If so, why the implicitly self-critical 'frozen' in the final lines: 'Frozen in a childhood pose,/I stand at the window, awaiting the blaze.' Could this be an indirect attack on the moral ambiguity of the *vita contemplativa*? Is the passive poet high up above the fire even meant to be perceived to be twiddling his thumbs like Nero? Or is the apparent invitation to interpret allegorically merely a subterfuge to flush out any surviving New Critic? Krüger has divulged in conversation that he was indeed thinking of Nero here, in particular of Orson Welles's Nero; but, being the opposite of a didacticist, he leaves the reader to his own devices. A major theme is that of interpreting a reality scarcely amenable to interpretation, not least because one is aware that 'the interpretation includes me' (p.101). The first collection contains the lines 'I keep catching myself,/each morning, giving my dreams a one-sided interpretation' (R 28) and, later too, it is not just the notes of a woman sitting next to the speaker at a lecture (p.125) which resist decipherment. Perhaps it is no coincidence that the world only seems easily 'readable' in moments of self-delusion ('misunderstood quotations effortlessly/opened the overcast sky'; AdE 42) or of sinister surrealistic whimsy, as when the River Isar in Munich is said to decode, 'without trouble', the secrets entrusted to it during the cold war (p.33).

The obverse of such unwillingness to foreclose discussion of reality is the pluralism of Krüger's poetics. While so many German poets, following the lead of Krolow and Höllerer, have plumped either for the short 'hermetic' or for the long 'open' poem, he – a translator of William Carlos Williams – has always written both, has always been (in Thom Gunn's sense) a poet of inclusiveness.[9] 'Dedication' begins 'There's room in this house for many things', and this credo is restated a decade later in *Eine alte Geschichte II* ('An old story II'): there is still space in his head, an ungallantly juxtaposing narrator states, for (among other things) an insect that thoughtlessly thinks itself at the centre of the universe, for you, for washed-up flotsam, Dignity, the flight of birds, for thesis, antithesis, for me....(D 100). The refusal to hierarchize experience means that the sublime ('no better, no worse/than the dirt on the ground' [D 101]), the grotesque, the base and the inconspicuous appear cheek by jowl. This is so both in terms of content – the *Diary-Poems* take in the German equivalent of the printers' union GPMU as well as the grating of the cosmos – and of diction: a poem that begins with archaic *gravitas* can easily end with a four-letter word (p.154). The poem becomes a sort of dragnet or is (to use Krüger's own metaphor) a form with which to do the rounds of the world in an attempt to put a couple of words in the right light (p.83). The dragnet may turn out to be badly torn; the very frequency of Krüger's poetological poems betrays his doubts about the worth of the enterprise. The Age of Prose, which Hegel prophesied, has darkly dawned; lyrical poetry has, for Krüger, been a 'history of self-doubt' for more than a century (WuG 75-76).

A pessimist? Certainly; indeed, the repeated references to the 'end' of things – of the history of photography, of the Novel, of history itself – might make him seem, in Grass's sense, an adherent of 'finalism'.[10] From the start, Utopia is in its 'dotage', a thin, tremulous shadow that keeps as close as possible to our bodies as it *follows* us – the very reverse of Bloch's principle of *Vorschein* in *The Principle of Hope* (R 49). The Diderot glimpsed in *Diderot's Cat* has been worn out by his exertions in the service of the Enlightenment; where Freud, in *The Future of an Illusion*, optimistically argued that the illusion of religion would wither away as man gained control over nature, he has only hollow laughter for 'the ageing of an illusion' (p.47). In the novella *Wieso ich?* the father's guiding principle, 'Progress is the eternal recurrence of catastrophe', and his apothegm, 'We no longer have a history that is worth narrating, we've only got books to interrupt, for an instant, the process of self-deception' (*Wieso ich?* pp.16-17), both point in the same direction. Nor is 'The error that we are, that we/have won', a line from one of the *Diary-Poems*, an isolated eruption of despair (II 26). Yet it must be said that such pessimism relates above all to man, in particular to the elegiac, alexandrine world of knowledge. Animals (whether cats, birds, flies or snails) continually prove to be ideal anti-selves, and salvaging the quiddity of concrete things, however humble, is an act of self-redemption, a way of breaking out of the vicious circle of theoretical finalism.

Krüger's belief in creative man, in the power of the imagination in general, is at times reminiscent of Wallace Stevens (whom he greatly admires).[11] Perhaps the most paradoxical triumph of imagination occurs in 'Alive as a Dodo'.

For the Germans, whose language is without the expression 'dead as a dodo', the poem is doubly outlandish; the danger for Anglo-Saxon readers, on the other hand, is that they will conclude, after a cursory reading, that it is simply a statement of the ornithologically obvious. The text's easily overlooked optimism lies in the change in perspective (in section 4, the dodos themselves are allowed a retrospect on history), but above all in the unobtrusive manipulation of verb and tense: the bird's body only *seems* to have been lost for ever (section 1); that nobody *has seen* it since 1620 (section 5) is not the same as saying that it is extinct; the dodo *gets* (not: *was*) silenced by history (section 6). As though Krüger were turning Baudelaire's 'L'Albatros' on its head, the apparently grotesque creature turns out to be the 'bird of love': imagination (the poet's, or rather its own) allows it to reacquire a body, to speak prophetically, to emerge as a paragon of vision. What is most surprising about this *creatio ex nihilo* is not that it involves of all things, the unlyrical dodo but that – in view of the author's inveterate scepticism – it should come about at all. *Credo quia absurdum*: it says much about Krüger's implicit belief in the power of the *poetic* word that – in spite of his misgivings about language on account of its tendency to fill up, devour or displace the world it is allegedly describing – he should except poetry from a condemnation of the 'universal process of verbalization which is covering the earth like a canker', that he should still hope, against hope, that poetry may be able to 'interrupt' the indiscriminate flood of language (WuG 76).

The Swiss writer Adolf Muschg has compared Michael Krüger to 'a well-disguised mystic…a scribe who has got beyond books, to the point where the wisdom of masters begins – the absurd wisdom which writes its final word on water. It would not be entirely wrong, either, to call Krüger a master of the love-poem, a first-rate painter of landscapes and climates, a reviver of the Roman Elegy, a painter's poet. But he is all these things with a difference: there is a "remainder" which – in rational terms – should not exist, which one will only discover if one is not looking for it and which is…everything' (D 156). I hope that something of this *je ne sais quoi* survives in the following versions which are appearing to mark the author's fiftieth birthday in December 1993.

RD, Munich, 1993

xiv

Notes

1   Krüger's poetry is referred to as follows: *Reginapoly*, Munich: Heyne 1980 (= R); *Diderots Katze*, Frankfurt/M: Fischer 1980 (= DK); *Lidas Taschenmuseum*, Pfaffenweiler: Pfaffenweiler Presse 1981 (= LT); *Aus der Ebene*, Frankfurt/M: Fischer 1985 (= AdE); *Wiederholungen*, Berlin, Literarisches Colloquium 1983 (= W); *Stimmen*, Pfaffenweiler: Pfaffenweiler Presse 1983 (= S); *Die Dronte*, Frankfurt/M: Fischer 1988 (= D); *Welt unter Glas*, Stuttgart: Reclam 1986 (= WuG); *Zoo*, Pfaffenweiler: Pfaffenweiler Presse 1986 (= Z); *Idyllen und Illusionen*, Berlin: Wagenbach 1989 (= II); *Hinter der Grenze*, Pfaffenweiler: Pfaffenweiler Presse 1990 (= HdG).

2   *Den Kopf voll Suff und Kino* is the title of a nakedly confessional collection by Christoph Derschau, which came out in the same year – 1976 – as Krüger's first volume, *Reginapoly*.

3   'die *reinen* Füße sollen durch *Stolper*schritte unterbrochen werden, um das *Ohr* zu irritieren' (letter to the translator, 1.7.91).

4   'Sie haben zwar Vorbilder, die aber oft zu einem imaginären Bild zusammengezogen werden' (letter to the translator, 27.7.92).

5   E. Gombrich, *Art and Illusion*, 5th edition, London: Phaidon 1977, p.24.

6   Loc. cit.

7   Ibid., p.177.

8   S. Cramer, 'Ach, kleinmütiges Jahrhundert. Michael Krügers lyrisches Tagebuch „Idyllen und Illusionen"', *Süddeutsche Zeitung*, 6/7.5.1989.

9   T. Gunn, 'Adventurous Song: Robert Duncan as Romantic Modernist', *PN Review* 78 (1991), 21.

10 Krüger's 'Walk with a Philosopher', with its assumption that the end of history is nigh, came out in the same year as Grass's novel *Die Rättin*, in which the she-rat says: 'Finalism, the very last ideology, met with a favourable reception and attracted many adherents. People would casually say to their friends and acquaintances: "Do drop by again before it is too late." The going greeting was: "Nice to see you one last time." The expression "See you" was no longer used when one took one's leave' (G. Grass, *Die Rättin*, Darmstadt/Neuwied: Luchterhand 1986, p.74). On the other hand, the main speaker in the poem is meant to be Derrida.

11 If 'present' is substituted for 'past', a remark by Michael Hamburger on Stevens provides a suggestive starting-point for a reading of Krüger: 'However elusive as a whole, the past is a repository of fragments that are palpable to the imagination and can therefore be "shored against one's ruins"' (*The Truth of Poetry*, Harmondsworth: Penguin 1969, p.117).

from
Reginapoly (1976)

Dedication

1

There's room in this house for many things. For your bashful look
when you show surprise at its presence; for your
widely-travelled dreams in which I (finally) feature:
holding a fragment of glass up to the horizon and changing,
a tiny bit, the perspective or lying flat on the ground
(like a fragment of glass); for your absent gait, in the morning,
in between bathroom and kitchen: it will remain here for good,
will be visible, every fine morning, when morning's brightness
comes stealing in (the dark in disguise). That is for me,
unlike for you, a consoling thought: *a mode of progression
never to be effaced.* But I am (even now) more anxious,
more faint-hearted than you: which may explain these poems. I
used, for example, to be afraid that the house might be full,
full right to the gables with our stories, guarded by
my canine look. It's quite amazing how much fits
into this house! And *what* things fit! I recently saw myself
standing by the window, watching you enter the house.
Moments later, I heard myself phone and apologize –
stuttering, weary – for not having come. Heard myself hang up:
there's room for that sound too. Can you remember
the Chinese (?) folktale about the people who
wanted to capture a given note? You have to know what
one single note means in Eastern music. It's really a scandal
not to be able to free oneself from one's own embrace; not
to want to, you'd say. ('That his only remaining chance
was to *have* to save himself, not others, made
him occasionally happy.') My attempts to alienate myself
from myself, at least somewhat, have failed, at least so far;
I know. The process is complex, however, and not undangerous: will
never work when one's on one's own, and rarely when one's with one
other person; when several are there it is just conceivable. (There
are banal forms of jumping out of one's skin which I don't mean:
the last 150 years of philosophy are strewn with them: tactics as
ethics and ethics as tactics and so on and so on.)

2

There's room in this house for many things. For the misprints, for
instance, which litter my dreams and make of comeliness homeliness:
a co(s)mic catastrophe. Also for disorderly bliss
and the wanton, pagan disporting of cats. (I'm pleased, by the way,
that we call the cat cat.) It's soothing to sit here at this table
and stroll, a flâneur, in the *dark oubliettes of consciousness*;
in one's hand a glass globe in which it is snowing: there's room enough
    here
for return and departure. Naturally, it has got very hard
to have a thought of one's very own. But it should be natural,
too, to be able to keep it to oneself, entirely. It could fit
on this table next to the paper, there between the books and
the coffee-pot. Who is speaking? Allegedly, people know nowadays
who is. But that is naturally nonsense. Every movement,
every gesture is going to get harder. You know that. I'm cutting short
this Dedication here. *I* am. You know this trick and also know why
I'm resorting to it: even melancholics are occasionally hungry.

Preliminary Poem

Literature, I see myself write,
has got used to Misfortune (they
grew up together, telling each other
stories; later
they corresponded; at last, after many years
of mutual admiration, they made up their minds
to grow old together: recollecting
their childhood, the stories
of their childhood, which they could now
interpret). Got used to banal misfortune.
Desire. The narcissism of concepts.
The radiant metaphors for pain
and also for fear. To the pain of separation
as well as the fear of reunion. To
Repetition as well (which makes Literature confident
to take the stage even now, as though nothing at all had happened).
To all the mystifications and sweet tautologies.
To assumed names.
Just about: to the mirror, the duplicate,
the translation. But above all: to silence.
Literature paused.
She appeared lost in thought.
And wrapped herself in the coldest of silences.
Due to this break she could scarcely
be heard. Her stony silence
got her back into the gossip columns. She's speaking
again to attract attention. Much
she's forgotten, forgotten how to do, lost; and much
has been wrested from her. And yet,
I see myself write, she continues
to have her say.
There on the worn pad, between coffee-stains
and notes that are smudged and the telephone-numbers
of Revolution,
it's possible once again, she claims
(and others claim),
to collect, to placate
the breakneck movements.

Why there? And why only there? And
why placate? Sceptically
you look at the white sheet of paper, your hand, the pad in question;
as though as a matter of course, you've removed
every single book. You carefully classify your dreams –
they will later appear, as proof,
as illustrations. (You're shocked
at their unequivocalness, appalled
how much they resemble daydreams; already
you feel caught red-handed and fear
the unexpected visit you long to take place.)
As proof, as illustrations, of what?

The house. The window. The view.
A particular light. None is yours.
This you have read.
This you have learnt. And seen
as a possibility, but not accepted
as a condition.
This doubt, too, you can read up about: it is part
of the problem. What, then, is yours?
Perhaps the beginning? Perhaps
this single second in which you pick up
the pencil? (For later: this second
is not yours either!) Perhaps
your experience of the unpleasant side
of language? (That would be precious little; and others
have got to suffer far more due to theirs.)
You suddenly feel the desire to survive:
'hibernate': hoping
for better days. In the hope
that something will be yours later (it
never will). You cannot stop jumping up
and rushing across to the window. Is this view your own?
This image? The movement
you make as you pull the curtain to?

And thus you write, I see myself write,
about alien property. You are writing
on revolutions, rebellions, changes,
reforms. You are writing about a man
who's constantly jumping up and rushing across to the window,
about what he sees: he sees, you write, I see
myself write, two Turks raking up
dead leaves and tossing them on to a car

while the driver, presumably
a German, is reading the paper. He hits the roof,
you write, and quickly closes the curtains
so as not to have to bear the sight
any longer. You write with the utmost concentration
about the dazed state of the world
and about a man
who turns his innermost self inside out
and, all of a sudden, discovers something he thought
had been lost. The loss, you write, I see myself write,
had a very practical value: the fact
that the thing turned up again made him depressed. Then
you draw fine lines between the man
at the window and the introvert, between
the dazed state of the world and
the two Turks. You try
to create a balance between all
parts, and fail. Why are you
vexed? Is it really your fault? It's hope-
less, you write, I see myself write,
to write about the world: the 'laws
of succession' drive me right round the bend. You're
on an enormous sheet of paper.
With wide-open eyes you drive up and down
the frontier, and then discover the house,
the window, the view, a particular light.
Laughing, you make all things cry. On the left:
the mirror, the duplicate, the translation; and on the right:
the revolutions, rebellions, changes.
Before me, the white sheet's infinitude,
is what you report: I make a note, for
later. Towards a poem
on the writing
of poems.

On the Stairs

Dearth, she recounts,
has got stout: on protein,
cinema, farinaceous food;
too many short cuts, too lofty goals.
He has moved and
feels bored
in his new apartment.
Is making up stories
now for sitcoms: an eye
for an eye. When asking questions,
his voice is deep;
but he rarely speaks.
He's grumpy, obese.

My Ear

1
Sunday afternoon. Awaking from
a siesta of sorts, I found the door
ajar – which made me think of my
ear. Far from rested, I hunted for
my face on the wall. Before sleep
came, I had clapped both hands
to my ears and pondered a sentence
(from a lecture from the previous day):
'The history of photography
is at an end.' I wanted to keep
this sentence in mind, chemically pure,
detached from all the rest
that followed, on past
the end.

2
My aim was
to picture the final photograph:
were people on it?
Was some bit of nature? Which and/or who?

A portrait? In the foreground, I thought,
a portrait of contemptuousness: self-
satisfaction in the gaze,
and nervous light; a polemical poem
on beginnings. The background would be
a report on the rapid spread
of hysteria. On the afternoon
in question, the history
of photography came to an end. I quickly
rose and slammed the door to,
in order to destroy the image of my
ear.

3
The irony was that things had started off
so well: the eye's excitement, the concentration,
the unmoved contemplation of the
swiftly flowing tears; soft focus.
Another ending. In this century's
final quarter, this maddening
madding. I anxiously fingered
my ear, its velvety cartilage: we will
learn, once again, how to hear: the din
of the swiftly flowing tears
a moment or two before
numbness sets in.

4
Until night fell, I stayed there, lying
utterly still on the bed,
my hands beside my thighs,
and thought of the end of the history
of photography. (There's much to be said
for theories that spring from resignation:
they cast long shadows in which
one can rest.) On the wall,
I suddenly saw a thin little man
in a shabby fur-coat; in front of him,
a girl with pigtails, tears
running down her cheeks – so slowly
that one could scarcely, scarcely perceive them.

Before the Meal. Four in the Morning

I've never yet eaten on my own, all myself,
she said, have never yet had the feeling of having
taken a meal independently. First there was Mother
(she said as she stood there in front of the fridge) who not only

stood at my side and wielded my spoon, determining
how and what and how much I should eat, but who also
was there in the food itself. I only ate to give
pleasure to Mother. She wasn't just there in the food, in

the dishes, but – increasingly – was the food itself.
My mother, she said – standing there in front of the open
fridge in a nightdress, freezing – was, as it were, my
daily bread. Which explains how thin she is, so she

claimed, her total inability to keep food down;
as well as her total lack of interest in certain foods.
In restaurants, for instance, the feeling of being in a
museum, the feeling of standing entirely outside

the natural order: her greed in restaurants, the manic wish
to order everything coupled with the grim awareness
that she could not even begin to pick at a single
thing. Her exultation when faced with rotten meals in

inns: had I noticed? I had no intention
of being drawn. Had *I* been forcibly struck as well
by the desperate loneliness of diners, especially
of fat ones, throughout the whole eating process, by their

attempts to fill themselves to the brim, attempts
that are doomed? The inability to put
the mess of dishes in apple-pie order reminded her
of museums too: greed, she went on, is due to a

rage for order or, rather, to a quite unappeasable
rage for order. The wide-open eyes are a pointer here:
eyes in search of a system which they, of course, will not
find. I, for example, just cannot eat with my eyes

closed, she said: the notion of not being able to see
what I'm eating brings on attacks of vertigo, peri-
stalsis cuts out automatically, even if I've
seen the waiter bringing the meal, that he's really

11

brought it. She was ice-cold. I: You have got very thin
of late. She: In critical situations, I always,
now, put on weight; the very presence of
others makes me swell up. They are all attempting un-

consciously to gorge me; surrendering, losing
weight would be out of the question in such situations;
at such times I feel unfortified. (And years ago?)
I'd
have slimmed down at once, would (so to speak) have dispersed myself;

everything used to flow out of me – quite noticeably.
I could literally see how everything flowed away
out of me. In critical situations, she used,
at once, to become as thin as a rake. Like now,

I said. Suddenly it was light outside.
The fridge was open, as before; it was very cold. You're cold,
I said. She replied: the whole complex business of eating,
the mumbojumbo of eating, the thrills that it used

to give me now, in retrospect, send a shiver
down my spine; I stole into the kitchen
in order to learn how to eat. Admittedly, that sounds rather
odd. Utopia is keeping one's weight

when the going gets rough. I'd like to keep mine
when the going gets rough, and that's why I'm here.
I want to surrender nothing and to assimilate
nothing; I want to be impregnable and very round.

That is one's only hope, she maintained, trembling
with cold. A round glass body in which one can
watch the process of digestion and that of
decomposition, excretion, without the body

altering: I'm well on the way to achieving that state.
I can't understand why such things hold so little interest
for people. Why, she asked, has it all been forgotten?
I put all the hotplates on and began with the preparations.

Diderot, I said, getting down to peeling potatoes –
something in Diderot – craved potatoes on his deathbed, a
truly polemical wish in the history of civilization.

                                        (for Fred Oberhauser)

Looking around a finished building
on the way to a South German lake

I'm no longer scared to death, she suddenly said
on the way to Bad Wiessee, during a truly grand
thunderstorm on the autobahn:
I'm no longer scared to death of all the internal
explosions, the claps of thunder that furrow my heart;
what gives me the jitters is this quite infinite stream
of letters, this murmur of infinity
inside my head: because I don't know
at which point I should leap to my feet since each clause
keeps on entailing subordinate clauses;
I'm scared of the terrible uniformity of language,
scared of the fact that it can't be interrupted in spite of
eruptions, explosions and revolutions. It drives me mad:
this invisible influx into my head,
this invisible efflux – because I cannot
plan any longer, because the outcome is always
as old, as pathetic, as we are, because
I cannot say: stop; this crazy helplessness
blighting all letters is making me crazy,
at any rate nervous. We can turn round,
I said, by the lake there is only water and trees
and unbearably excellent air, but as I said this
I squinted hard in the driver's mirror and,
motivelessly, went up into fourth. When I write
a sentence, I can't stand how long it takes
to do so; I want to explain this right away,
then comes the explanation of the explanation,
etc. etc. You know what I mean:
what I've in mind is a giant structure
of sentences, explanations and footnotes,
a sturdy total sentence, a kind of domestic sentence
in which I can live and which lives in me and fills me completely.
With halls and galleries, suites of rooms and stairs, with gigantic
flights of outdoor steps, you see, where my tribunals
take place, where I say: *you* stand behind the barrier here
and *you* there in front, where an ancient bar will separate
the narcissistic opponents, where there's, for ever, a draught.
There's no such thing as structural fatigue: things and gestures
and language etc. are subject to the strictest
of checks. (And my room:) Is high up in the attic;
your look is free to range right over the provinces.

I have to laugh. Something is hurting beneath my spleen,
and in my head a familiar burning pain: something is happening
now, I can sense a quite distinct strain,
a distant scraping, an uninterrupted
journey through every single organ; no commentary.
After we'd just left the autobahn, the thing I'd feared
happened: I, she said, am working on
a machine with which to obliterate
history – startled phantasms, dreams,
you see, but also the gradual transitions, the cerebral
scandals, the imbecilities of nature simply
get burnt up. The ash is a kind of special
manure for my gardens on the horizon, obtained
on a low flame: natural, nutritive. O please do
shut up. That's childish. Like your childish delight
when the little red lamps start flickering, like your whole
machine thing, your house. Okay, but language, the uninter-
rupted language of civilization, of culture, the
so-called language of nature and then my house, this
splendid edifice raised in the middle of the river,
interrupting its flow; go on, please do say
yes. If you say yes, I'll abjure all machines.

Winter Poem

The damp in the works. The faint-hearted dread
of the rust. The wet clothes,
the joints full of twinges; the sodden skin:
rain, thank goodness – Nature's
adapting. We talk at breakfast
of Death, of its daring operations,
of its adaptability. We talk
of its changed physiognomy
as shown in the photo in the paper,
taken in a department store
in the city-centre, after it had got away.
Is *that* what Death looks like? No one's
annoyed at the damp-stained salt. The eggs
have always tasted of fish-meal,
says a man who's incessantly running to the window
out of distrust of the doorbell. Quickly
change the subject: this Death
was not our invention either.

The conversations that come to nothing. Discussions about
their abortiveness which we glean
from the paper: an era is over. An era
of witty playing on words and
of startled faces, of waxing
world. The Future is sitting freezing at his writing-table,
someone exclaims, caressed and caressed by Progress
until his back is crooked. A clapped-out eccentric
clutching on to his tea-cup; I know him
from the old days. The old days. Someone else
has flung open the window so we can hear
the rain deep in winter: as though off his trolley,
he tries to describe the sound that rain makes.

The inefficiency of dreams. So many selves.
And so much tea to get through the morning
during this winter
which seems to us so very unyielding
(despite the rain). Image-production
is falling off, the machine's 'spluttering':
its lovely regularity, its economic
benefits, its gentle rattling
that used to wake us up in the morning, its

15

unrestricted movements have slowly ground
to a standstill. The greatest invention
in the history of deception, someone remarks,
has destroyed itself.

The dejection of things. The taste
and the hue of Illusion, and its immutable
substance, its time-honoured ways
of whipping up panic: that would be worth
describing, together, after a walk;
we'd be doing our bit
to ensure the survival of precision. The observation
of the dying of a movement
of the hand or the head; the noting
down of that observation in the teeth
of one's dread of blank paper, in the teeth
of the cranky dictate of usefulness.
After that, the man who distrusts the doorbell says,
we'd have outwintered winter.

Out of humour

It's become hard
(is becoming harder)
to reach the present:
too breathless, too blind. My
letters all reach the person
who sent them. It's become hard
to dare to try
to speak. I am speaking:
so deep is the chasm
separating us from the future.

Archaeology

1
All year long ('75) I was out
to write a political poem on

Germany; it was to be called The Unnatural
Warmth, and was intended for a friend in

California who could not make it to
Germany that year, who could not travel

through Germany in the year in question
to see for himself all the things that had changed:

the poem was to have filled the gap
between what was, then, his most recent stay

and his next, to prevent him from taking fright
when he next came, from taking the next plane back,

or from having to hurry to check his ticket
to see, for example, whether he'd landed

somewhere else. All year long I gathered
material for The Unnatural Warmth

concerning the unnatural warmth that had spread
through Germany: in the papers and journals,

in houses and flats and out on the
streets, in people's heads and in discussions

about the great cold they said had spread
in the papers and journals, and out on the

streets, and in houses and flats, and in discussions,
and in people's heads. On the first of each month

I got down to sifting through the notes
towards my meteorological poem:

the notes on the wind which, suddenly violent,
had turned against us; and on the rapidly

spreading depression and on the concomitant
change of weather; the cold sea-air from South-Western

Europe they said should have blown north-easterly;
on all the climactic fluctuations and other meteoro-

logical shocks. I was out to attempt
to describe the fear that was spreading, the fear

of the cold-spell forecast and what that fear meant:
that everyone suddenly huddled together

to warm each other; and suddenly got
all wrapped up, beyond recognition almost;

that hardly anyone graced the streets;
that the few who did were glued to the sky,

interpreting cloudscapes; that, as a result
of the fear of the cold-spell that had been forecast,

summer in Germany felt like December.
People are whispering as in winter, I noted, and yet

the sun is beating down hotter than ever. It was to have been
a poem on the spread of the power of meteoro-

logy and on its demonstrably incorrect forecasts.

2
At the end of the year, on 16.12.1975,
the bag with my notes was stolen at Tegel

Airport. I sat there, morose, in a hotel
in Littlehampton, on England's south coast, opposite

Europe; outside it was cold and pouring with rain.
I spent my time wondering whether, for climatic reasons,

they'd changed the course of the Gulf Stream. Un-
interruptedly, I read German papers that all arrived

appallingly late. In Germany archaeology
had been rediscovered, so I read; I thought un-

interruptedly of my poem. Blimey, can time
really pass that quickly. The archaeology of the opera. The

archaeology of the cinema. My major political poem
on Germany: up the spout. I tried to imagine

gigantic excavation-sites in Germany –
the Rhine-Main Region dug up completely,

and Baden-Württemberg one big black hole. The archaeology
of the Future. The year which had just passed was also judged

in terms of all sorts of archaeological
factors. A very odd business. My year,

the year of my projected poem. Oddly enough,
there were few overlaps. Regarding the climate,

all the commentaries differed from my
observations, for instance. Or take another fact

that featured in none of the retrospects: in '75
Fascism had been thirty years dead (or maybe not).

Instead a long list of dead individuals everywhere:
white-haired men and women with faces furrowed

by care. I flew back as fast as I could to Berlin
to search on the spot for my manuscripts:

the poem I'd planned would indeed fill a gap
in the market, if it did get written,

or so I thought. But, when disembarking,
a voice in me said: you'll never find your bag with the notes,

never again. It was hellish cold there in Berlin,
the ice-bound flat was especially

unbearable: muffled in pullovers, blankets, I crouched
beside the window and crossly mused

on the loss of my poem and on the curious
boom in archaeology in Germany.

Postliminary Poem

The signs are speaking
a different language:

they've every right to.
We thought that their
ambiguity
was as safe as houses,

and now are offended,
tight-lipped. Once again

we're sitting there stranded
in alien chairs and rooting,
resigned, in paper-filled lairs. There's
reason, no rhyme, now in many things:

rich rhymes that, several years back,
would have seemed like slips of the tongue.

from
Diderots Katze (1978)

1

As of this morning
the travel agency is closed.
(The owner, they say, has robbed
the till and made a quick getaway.)
Through the window I watch
the jerky peregrinations of the flies.
They're studying timetables scrupulously:
Greece, Spain, Morocco, Switzerland.
While I'm still annoyed about what's (not) on offer,
they take off.
Are already sitting helplessly
on foreign beaches or neckdeep in snow.
Some are unable to make up their minds.
They stay glued to Germany,
to the Black Forest,
and soon die, like flies.

2

The seasons
sluggishly flow apart.
November, as though in a sub-standard film;
and, in December,
next year's sullen April
is stirring.
Nevertheless heavy downpours
come as a terrible shock.
We expect the birds to return any time now.
We have no problems
this winter, claim the refuse collectors,
but there are more unemployed. The houses
are all that seem to be cleaving still to the
old calendar. Sourly, morosely, they're
freezing away, and rising in price.

3

The newsstand
feels shame at the repetitions.
The more State, I mean the more enemies,
the greater the honour. Each day
new values are being discovered. Yesterday: Tenderness.
Now, today: Love in the broadest sense.
How things have changed, have not changed. Each day
a brand-new sweater, distracting attention
from the face.
My neighbour has taken to wearing shades.
He's out to revive the sonnet
this winter. We'll see, he says,
we'll see if the old form's still viable.

4

Glacial cold
at the butcher's. Quaking,
the sausages gorp at me, miles of pale meat.
Is the average family getting larger?
Are there more pets?
Shaking, a liver changes hands,
and later a heart.
And all in exchange for good German money.
No, we're not going to go to Mallorca,
we're staying at home. In Germany,
where the roses blow.

5

Last stop: the post-office.
Long queues: many familiar faces;
a nodding and waving;
no one dares to fall out of line. The woman in front
is frantically holding her letter
face-down, but keeps on checking,
checking if the address is still right.
(Later I read that the letter
is bound for Karl-Marx-Stadt. Aha!)
When it's my turn I somehow don't want to
send off my telegram any longer.

6
In the middle of the road
a man drops a parcel
and then pretends that he did it on purpose.
He stands there triumphant. He's waiting,
I think to myself, for the interest
to die down again.

7
Back home, I leave the door ajar;
it's possible, after all, that you'll come.
I can wait.
I can wait.
The shadow's acute at one o'clock
at this time of year.
The telephone rings –
the ringing will soon rip the house to pieces.
(What will they find in the ruins, I wonder?)
Warily I lift the receiver
and then keep silent.
'All speech contains a grain of contempt.'

8
And that's the way that winter looks this year.
The longing grows and grows, the days first wane,
then wax.
No, no, my soul,
there is no helping me.

My new apartment: 'period' house

A different floor,
an entirely new world:
defeats take place in ground-floor flats.
And a single pigeon
brings disaster upon
the thin sky which
flies off, squawking.
Every shadow a genuine tragedy:
in these houses,
sheltered and swindled,
one has the right –
at one's own cost and risk –
to decline, to die.

My new apartment, Liebigstr. 7

                    Here,
in Liebigstraße
                in Lehel
in the old part of Munich,
quite suddenly, two Indians die.
One was a newspaper-vendor;
                        at night
he'd do the rounds of the public houses,
clad in a crimson plastic-
jacket and with a quite
impossible accent.
Without being asked
                    he'd put the papers
on the tables,
                politics
face-down. Everyone had to
touch, then buy, a paper; it was
a ritual
                        just like
eating roast pork and
drinking beer.
                    Where you come from?
the people would ask
who left the change lying there
in this Bavarian leprosy ward.
                            Let's have a guess!
Sometimes I'd see the Indians
at the pensioners' duels
                        down by the river,
the old women bent on feeding the pigeons
while the old men, slyly,
                        behind their wives' backs
brandish and brandish their walking-sticks
until the pigeons and gulls take off,
with a whirring of wings, and carry the wives
across to the *Deutsches Museum*
or, if the wind should change,
to the *Haus der Kunst*.

When that happened the Indians laughed.
Now they are being collected, removed,
in two metal coffins.
The pensioners: once again out and about,
the women with little bags of rice,
the men with their sticks –
their vigorous stride
on the way to the river.

Sunday, 15.1.78, 4.30 p.m.

A walk
comes to grief.
Not a soul
on the streets.
No snow.
Between things:
a gloomy, grey absence.

The last inhabitants
have, this minute,
left the quarter.
Little
remains.

All that holds up
the houses
is a Bavarian sky;
white veins
are protruding with the strain.

Then, at last,
the houses fall down.

In which stratum, then,
will we take our long rest?

There down beneath us:
war materials; what remains
of Reconstruction;
small warmth-giving ideas
that are made of mouldable matter.

A sturdy bed
for the imprint
of our rudely felled bodies.

Our
coverlet, though,
will be flimsy,
not cosy: child's play
for the archaeology
of the future.

On days like this
it is senseless to act
as though, on the morrow,
a new day begins.

After Work

On the way home,
I cross the Tivoli Bridge
each day.
I love
the river's
wrinkly face
with the wet, white
veil of haze
above it, the slithery railing;
the gulls are misplaced.
This is the way that I picture the future:
a river that mumbles perpetually
without full-stops or commas,
purified, cleansed and
sallow and stinking and
full of desire for
the limpid waters
of the spring thaw.
And full of white birds.

From the other bank of the River Isar,
correspondents of Radio
Free Europe approach:
Poles, Romanians, Russians.
When I get too near them,
they suddenly switch to English
or else fall silent, let slip,
abashed, their secrets
which, without trouble,
the river decodes.
Eddies result, hissing punctuation
pointing
the discourse, the fluent discourse,
upon the future.

The cat is dead

I found her
next to the dustbin
stiff
after a supple life.

Strange,
she was lying on her belly
with paws outstretched.

It was in this position
she'd lie in front of me
when I was prompted to read to her.

What caught her fancy
were old travel books.
She knew, for example,
by heart the true story
of Oblomov's voyage
round the world.
(As is well known,
this Czarist official
did not go ashore a single time
in the whole of the journey.)
Outlandish things
held no appeal,

I said to her
when she was keen
to slip off at night.
She frequently
treated me
like a child.

But when I actually
acted like one,
she'd instantly
bristle.

Errors, lack of attentiveness
she'd correct
with a courteous
quiver of whiskers.

Each of us
led a double life –
she at night
and I in the daytime –
which we hid from one another,
sedulously.

Only of late
did she hint that I was to
be let in on
her fur-warm life

as a reward
for patient observing.
Now she has died
in the posture of listening.

And I feel
the victim.

On Hope

Hope
we wanted to take unawares
as she lost her composure:
right in the second of revolt.
We braced ourselves
for a pretty long journey,
arming ourselves
against heat and cold.
The rations
weighed heavily on our shoulders:
history, upbringing,
also the power to cope with
hopelessness, yards of books.
We got back sometime yesterday.
Weary,
as you can perhaps imagine,
and more than just peckish.

The pictures
have not yet been developed.
The findings
will be announced in due course.

Love Poem 3

We watch ourselves
go down the winding stairs –
you count the even ones
and I the odd.
It smells of wax here;
to descend is easy
(tea grows insipid,
stoves grow slowly cold).
Emptiness here allures;
the light goes out –
a hollow plopping sound –
goes on again:
the final film of strangeness –
blown away.
The tracks of thinking lead
straight to the heart.

Out in the open air
the soul grows wings;
the dream is over –
heads again rule things.

Without a Word

They are conversing about the unfitness
of the solutions,
those men down there outside my window.
This is abundantly clear
from their gestures:
importunate, foolish,
unmistakably impatient.

They're writing books with looks
and using the street as their source.

As though in a fit, they're tearing sentences
into shreds: the argument's
dangling there from one arm, the proof
is lodged in the crook of the other.

How much egg there is on their faces!
What ceremony are they standing upon?

The fighting is over,
the text continues. Now, in relief,
they're shaking each other's hands,
the men there outside my window.

That is the starting-point of their novel.
But that's not what matters.

From above

About four o'clock:
a man is gathering the horizon.
He's riding a bicycle
so as to keep right up with the sun.
Another, on foot
and far, far away,
hasn't an earthly –
from my perspective.
While the one,
bent over the handlebars,
is reaching the village,
the other is gulped up by the dark.
It is now five.
The truth of this hour
has truly avenged
the plundered look.

A brief reminiscence of summer

1
If we don't look at it, who will hold
this nervous picture together? The eye
encircles the open sky, rounds up

the fugitive clouds, creating
order. It guards both colours
and things: supervises

an azure wall behind which lurks
a concept with a masterkey
for forms not visible to the eye,

that's to say the informer who leaves
his fingerprints in this history of a
moment.

2
Such twinkling moments, in the biography of our senses,
are rare now. For a dislocation
has taken place and must be allowed for.

But in what language? The sky, it is true,
is still discussing aerodynamics.
The clouds are retailing a Turkish folktale.
Though the concept is discreet, we're clear
on its motives. That leaves the eye. It's
beside itself: business is bad.

The laws that govern trading in looks
are changing daily, and hourly
the light is changing its words.

3

Then, in the evening, people return. Some
sit, disguised, on benches in the market-
place while others, in front of the church, are out

to make Time stand still with their walking-sticks.
The beach is now empty, capfuls of wind. A daring wave
breaks just short of the shore, the next one

drags itself, crackling, on to the dry land, and then dries up.
The eye begins to study silence.
Who was I then? And who am I here?

The Path into Pictures

We gathered, mistrustful,
in the poorly lit museum:

a rumour had roused us
to look, with fresh eyes, at a picture there.

All of a sudden we glimpsed a hole in the
upper left-hand corner of this original, glimpsed
an inconspicuous passage there
in the midst of most sumptuous countryside:
the picture pictures
Paradise.

(On all the copies known to us,
in Venice, London, Leningrad,
the passage is veiled
by the uniform shade of a chestnut-tree –
is invisible to the naked eye.)

(Of course all attempts
to blow this minute aperture up
were completely in vain.)

After we'd studied a now forgotten
theory of perspective (Padua, 1639), we resolved
to attach the greatest importance
to the passage in question
which simply refused to be reproduced.

It was unbelievably cold in that place.

We got down to work without witnesses.

(The attendants, in the last century, used
to gather around an electric stove
and, in whispers, lamented
the death of lifelike art, lamented

Man's disappearance.)

Those who, like us, take the trouble to send
their gaze through the dripping-wet passage
will glimpse
a slippery, dusky path kept in place
by pebbles from a different age.

The path has been cut through a landscape
that we'd like to style 'rugged':
karst and meagre vegetation.

The non-horizon
suddenly struck us,
the fact that the light was limitless.

And slightly later we noticed too
that we had not moved.

Where this precarious path peters out,
a path of the eye,
a city stands in a sphere
of consummate isolation.

The name of this city is: At the End of Photography.

And in it,
the centre of Repetition,
lit by uniform light
and enwombed in uniform heat,
the pictures survive.

And in a fantastical factory
(built from the blurred edges inwards,
completely translucent)
the fragments the pictures took from the world
get collected, connected.

Here each gesture recovers
a motive, each panic its cause.

The most inconceivable metamorphoses
(drawn from the history of illusion)
encounter their daring biography here.

In this city
(that knows no present, only a past
and a future that is more than uncertain)
an order obtains that
destroys
our gaze
grown accustomed to our century.

The city At the End of Photography
proves a city of alien pictures.

On the outskirts
(on our way back)
we finally come across some people:
hanging up to dry in trees
and gently moving to the tune
of a totally alien concept of drama.

These pictures will survive all right:
cut-off, shielded, bathed in bright light
and in uniform heat,
they're preserving the history of passions,
of gestures, and of the gaze,
the felicitous insult.

They're there behind the original
of Paradise,

in the white centre of Repetition.

(for Floris Michael Neusüß)

Diderot's Cat
Photographed by Gabriele Lorenzer

Diderot at the window: at his side the cat —
her scaly fur in the bright window-frame.

Man, the machine, he explains to her
in a toneless voice: the rudiments
of physiology, intellect,
the violent workings of nature too.

He quotes the proceedings
of the Academy of Sciences for the year 1739
where mention is made of a man
without veins, without a heart.
On page 590, he adds with a hollow laugh,
caressing the fur of his cat
not without embarrassment.

Some photographs have a longer history
than photographic history does.

The cat watches closely as a cloud
travels briskly past in the
upper third of the window, too briskly:
her reflex reaction is panic-stricken.
Diderot, ground down by thirty years' labour
towards the *Encyclopédie*
is speechless:
the vehement dialectician admires
the simple grammar of nervousness.

A dog's whole soul resides in its snout,
he says, an eagle's in its eye,
a mole's in its ear. Diderot wonders
whether or not he ought to continue.

Man's soul, he starts again
— and breaks off
                    (soullessly cool,
the cat is writing a treatise on the influence
of the climate on the muddy
glass);
            (Diderot's watching
the revolution from the window, its gingerly
steps);
            an eccentric couple:
Diderot and the cat
in the badly cracked window-cross:
his fear of imitating her movements,
her mild polemic against his theory
of the machine.

We walk so little
work so little
and think so much, says Diderot,
that man in the end
will be nothing but head.

It's Sunday afternoon:
a good time
to remember emotions;
it's cold in Paris,
extremely quiet;
it comes home to Diderot just how hard
it is to smuggle his knowledge to safety.

Thirty years' labour towards the *Encyclopédie*
and still the machine's not working
the way it should. He gingerly probes
the bones, the bone-structure, of his cat.

We'll prove the first barbarians,
he suddenly says, the lachrymose tone
in his voice loud and clear.

His hollow laughter laments the ageing
of an illusion. The cat is contented.
Squinting, she's contemplating
the dust beside the window
and couldn't care less
that Reason knows no moderation.

Diderot admits defeat.
He glumly shuffles across to his desk
and notes down the following:
Where do I come from?
What did I use to be previously?
What is the point of my present existence?
What kind of life is awaiting me?

In what sort of frame will my fate
recreate me?
I have no answers.

He runs to the window
and – after a quick look down at the
street – begins to brood.

Only much later,
after the cat, with a mighty leap,
has freed herself
from the picture's cramping, constricting frame,
does he add serenely:

Philosophy too is instruction
in dying.

The Felony
Didactic Poem for Brecht's 80th Birthday

We've got to make
the leaves fall faster
We'll take the risk
We've got no choice but to fell
the tree at one fell swoop
We'll take the risk
We urgently need
the earth underneath
We appreciate that
Those who hesitate ought to consider:
Lofty Nature alone
will remember what befell.
We're risking the Fall.

Dear Erich Arendt,

When will you phone again? When can I hear your travelling voice
on the crackling line once again? (The voice
which has mastered Misfortune like a profession
one's forced to take up. One hundred and fifty terms of Progress
up at Hope's universities, and still
no degree. Where do you get your staying-power from, your
almost placid determination?)

When will you phone again, Erich Arendt? When can I hear
your poet's voice once again? (A voice
thick with resistance in spite of its shyness; with frequent brief pauses
for the interpreters in the exchanges. A southern
voice from Wilhelmshorst, Prussia, trained on a quite different
time-scale in places menacing our memory.)

When will you phone again, Erich Arendt? When the historians
go to confess, with their newspaperfaces? Their tiny
quadrangular cases full of small shot and shit,
their propagandamasks and badly fitting
suits that hide abysses of ignorance. Please do phone soon!
The present is livid at your quiet voice,
at your constancy in the slowsand of years.

We can see each other in Spain, if you wish,
in Barcelona or in Madrid. I'll take your works with me,
will read out your verses in the café. Dear Erich Arendt,
we could have never dreamt up such a world!
The lethal bite and yet: unscathed skin;
the sheerest contempt for the blaring rule of the head
and yet: an indefatigable head describing happiness.

When will we finally meet again? And
what is the pattern that governs our meetings?
Good to know you've a room here too –
made, it is true, of powerless words, but solidly built.

With Paul Wühr to the Styrian Autumn Festival

1

A revocable look from the window
of the car bound for Graz:
we can take a different route
when driving back to Munich,
if we survive
that is: his towering fear
in the mirror,
framed and pinned down: a feast
for the backseat-driver eager to talk poetry
in the course of this journey by eye
to Graz. Paul Wühr at the wheel
and me there behind him; the muttering tail-light
in between the mountains of books;
my powdery scoffs at the endless mountains
that rise out there in the 'freedom' of nature.
We cannot get out now, we've got
to drive on now, we've got to get through,
get through the mountains, we must get to Graz.

2

The heavens empty; a slippery flight
in third, in throttled panic,
to Graz.
Paul, the manichaean, both the light and the darkness,
a feast for the gods
of Apostasy, Refusal. Paul Wühr
stepping on it, and
hitting the brake with a text in his head,
one that he frantically wants to remember,
not to lose to Nature
flitting there past the window,
speaking a different language to his,
an artificial grammar composed of dripping colours.
He suddenly shouts: A different language!
now as the twilight starts to fall,
a language of plenty, fandango, and makes
the car dance, sheer madness,
he shouts, and drives us on to Graz.

3

In Graz. Safe in Braun's Tavern, he says
something about the beginnings of language,
the end of the world, to the girls. The bashful
Apocalypse buff inducts them
into the fine art of prophecy; and the upshot
is laughter, more wine,
and also his way, which defies imitation,
of tirelessly telling about the earthquakes,
the floods, the most dreadful devastations
of language. Even as he pays,
he's preparing our exit, trying out
the 'other voice': we've got to make tracks,
he calls, get the hell out. Paul on the run:
muffled in his dialect,
he stands there in the night-bound street.
Anti-Graz, he calls, the night is masquerading.
He doesn't see it, is back at home
with his papers which rustle him into the open,
across into Freedom.

4

On the way back: the gentle Paul Wühr.
Not a word on literature, fellow-writers,
the inconspicuous sickness
of writing. Suddenly he acts as though
all were self-evident. He points out mountains
in the rear mirror; we stop three times
before the border. Here, I say, we nearly copped it
coming. Paul laughs.
I know the place by heart, he replies;
the swerve was just as inevitable
as brusquely changing direction can be
in the course of a poem.

On Longing

That is the long and the short of Longing?
The sum of the thing that, in the Age of Dissolution,
tears open suffering? Takes all the colour out of anger?
That's its biography?
These few crumbs on the tablecloth?
This ashtray, unemptied?
This supermarket that groans on the shelves?
These phrases
made of torn-out time?

Nothing
but bag upon bag of nerves.
Nothing
but false taciturnity!

If only someone would enter the room!
Fling open the windows!
If only, in a throaty voice,
someone said: More future!

Longing, however, says nothing at all
in its documents.
Desire becomes blurred;
the word, its watery ink, just fades:
it's no longer able
to stick to things.

Some philologist grimly dreams
of the twilight, the night, of the libraries.

1
Humiliating
that this is not ours
People out in the free open air Green Germany
laid out put out at interest between all the little houses
And in the spring sunshine the heirs
are sitting outside their piles applauding nonstop
the downward trend in the rate of profit

2
Hope is swelling the River Neckar
the little boats digest every bend
Oh what stability! What sprezzatura!
If I'm not altogether mistaken
Life has good prospects
in between Munich and Stuttgart and back
if you are sitting facing the engine
all windows open and if the paper
rat-a-tattats as it leaves the compartment

3
The passengers try to vanish
in plush The witnesses: silent
A wan familiarity keeps us
in very vague touch with the world
racing past I'm making no headway
I'm not we're not in the train
that's going from Munich to Stuttgart and back
Students swap photocopies
of poems by classical poets
The pensioner there in the corner defends
his greatest hour with great bitterness
The victor has long since signed the verdict

4

Nobody wants to get out In Augsburg
or in Ulm All focus their thoughts
on the destination the terminus
The coffee-prices are climbing steeply while we
sit tight Two marks for powder and water
in cardboard An interesting life
I cannot call it anything else
Green Germany The curtains all filled
with the breath of Hope Thus you fly past us
We show our tickets and keep our mouths shut
Thus we get carried along and along

5

And back again later again not in danger
The thing that would save us grows somewhere else

from
Lidas Taschenmuseum (1981)

Paradise. Circa 1530

They are not saved:
neither by the perspective,
the veil,
nor their nakedness.
In the centre of the painting
lives an uninhabited heart
in the midst of the milling looks
of the beasts. Whom should it
give itself to? Birds are nesting
away in the frame, patiently waiting
for their appearance; holding its breath,
a fish is gaping at the angel.

Paradise is round
and boundless: the light
in the background knows
no source, and knows no object.
Indifferent, it lights
the way for itself
into a wood where, freezing,
it comes to rest beneath moss.

Here is the place
we looked for too long.
Here dwell Experience,
Hate, Calculation.
Here is the image
of what the future
took from the hands
of an angel of Order.

Sorrowful people, so it is said,
left the painting, waving,
naked, to the beasts left behind.

Caught in seduction's snare,
they laughed. Their laughter, it's said,
reverberated around the painting's hermetic circle,
making the glass
protecting this paradise
very faintly, yet audibly, tinkle.

Circa 1580

No one
owns up to this painting:
it changed hands
listlessly,
without going up in price.
Rid itself
of colour, frame,
time.
Did not contradict
the aristocracy's
bored looks,
nor the lubricious gaze
of the bourgeois.
Did not resist
the great big fingers
which rolled it up
like yesterday's paper.

I came across it
in Portugal, after the revolution,
in a provincial museum.
Blow away the dust
that is lovingly covering it
and you'll see,
encoded in allegorical form,
Virtù who is wearing a weary smile
on her way, her implacable way,
through the stony desert of Knowledge.

Circa 1610

The first draft is hanging in Amsterdam:
a farmstead in a village street, in crayon
with body colour over it. On the right
are whitethorn bushes, behind them a house
that blends into infinity,
into a grey sky which, stern
and choppy, is checking all borders.

This world needs no shade.
For it borrows its light from the blooms
of two trees, which give theirs up gladly.
This world needs no God:
the paper, or rather the grey priming colour,
speaks for itself, for the woodland path
which glumly fades away
as though it had never existed.

God has no place in this picture,
only a stiff-necked man. The latter
has just arrived, worn out
after walking all the way from the town.
Should he knock at the door of this ghost-house?
Should he stay where he doesn't belong?

The actual painting has been lost.
But we know from the very thorough study
'Inleyding tot de Hooge Schoole der Bilderkonst'
what it once looked like: no man
to be seen. A branch
that was leafless but laden with lichen stared,
long and hard, at the seeker, made history.

All this master's later paintings
attempt to bury the Netherlands
under a mountain of mountains;
as do the many preliminary sketches.

Circa 1630. A Skull

Where on earth can one put this painting?
It doesn't extol the myth
of Beauty,
nor that of Knowledge,
nor the myth of Cognition either.
It's not a symbol of Transience
and serves no anatomical purpose.
(The ancient Amsterdam Guild of Surgeons
scotched that presumption by selling the thing.)

It merely displays
a precisely painted skull
with clenched teeth.

What was the last word
to leave this mouth?

This head, without doubt, has
been around: the landscapes of Europe –
engraved on its bones.
So too Europe's wealth and weariness,
murders and ever-gnawing remorse.

Despite everything, this head
is neither an emblem of Failure,
nor of Falsehood. It's rigidly staring
west, to the left, towards the ocean
that links it with all things:
with the forgetfulness of continents,
growing, ever more quickly, on maps;
and with a reality
sinking and sinking inexorably.

We cannot forgive this skull, that was painted
around 1630, a single thing. Neither its origin,
nor its mien nor the things that it knows.
Until it's prepared to release the word
concealed in its jaw,
we'll keep on looking at it in silence
with firmly clenched teeth.

Circa 1640

A candle is burning away
in the mirror. (As to the skin
of the hand holding it,
it's as swarthy as leather.
The hand of a peasant,
blackened in the Thirty Years War.)

No eyes.
No nose.
No mouth.

A Caravaggiste
who has burnt Life up
with a single candle.

The light of this candle
has, for more than 300 years,
been locked in combat,
deep in a patient mirror, with Death.

No war
No doubt
No pity

were able to put it out.
Only the hasty breath
of Analogy made it flicker
on the swarthy, leathery skin
of the hand of a human being,
blackened in the Thirty Years Peace.

Circa 1700

A feeling
is touching the earth.
Narcissus
is looking, in vain,
for himself in the sand
which is wordless, unseeing,
smoothed
for Man's
advent.

Circa 1750

Three apples, two plums,
some kitchen utensils: Truth,
undivided, is bodied forth;
as in a show-case,
it lies there before you,
both untouched and untouchable.

You turn away
so as not to go mad.
Run off, like a thief,
possessing nothing
except the silence
that keeps on leaping
out of your heart.

19th Century

1

Nothing makes progress. And nothing endures. There's only this:
the angel's face, which is turned away,
and his arms which are flailing as he plummets,
his highly heroic attempt not to pave
the ground – the lovingly tiled floor of Europe,
which both attracts and repels and sustains him –
with his head first.
Only this faltering fall persists,
scaled down to picture postcard size
for the inside pockets of jackets: heart-high.
They've been restoring
the many-roomed museum for years.

2

Beyond the tiles, the field. The background
of the reproduction is closing,
grey; the path through the village
is fading; horses; hens; a dog
that, for years now, has frightened away its prey;
and tiny people who aren't looking up
as though they don't think
the angel will ever strike the ground.
None of these things can be seen any more;
and, until the museum reopens,
we won't be able to check
what it is that we want. That much is certain.

3

Dread all round,
and everything's quaking, fragmenting
round me, and at the century's
wriggling end a madman will sit
on the earth, supercilious, self-possessed,
swaddled in blankets like an Indio,
face turned away. Yes, he is writing!
Inscribing, with gout-ridden fingers,
the date of its death on the earth,

on its care-worn face. And now he is dying.
Yes, he is dying, purged of ambition,
legally incapacitated and spitefully sniggering
over the fall of the still falling angel.
That was long before the great storm
which swept out hearts, which sorted out minds,
which razed our bodies prior to the fall.

4
Nothing endures. And nothing makes progress. There's only this:
our look, that only seems to be moving.
Restlessly, it is gorping at the gloomy fellow
the background is, this moment, releasing;
a man with a hat on, in Sunday clothes
too black, too heavy, simply too lifeless
for this time of year. And fusty too.
Where, in this painting, does he fit in?
Nothing is different but nothing's the same:
no place, no black space, remains for this man
who, helplessly courteous, is coming on
beneath the hand of the falling angel.
For whose sake? And for what audience?
And what is the point of his standing there?
He goes, leaves the painting.
We see him later in the town,
a ruffled bird which is wearily cawing,
pursued by the children on its way
to the (still closed) museum.

5
Do not be anxious, future heart,
never was there more outset than now
with the copies printed.
And, one fine day, the museum will open –
instead of the paintings, there'll just be thin air,
and one shining mirror on every wall
to reflect your face in the panic moment;
mirrorrorrorred a thousand times, a single shriek
in the second the angel strikes the ground.

from
Aus der Ebene (1982)

On the Bridge

The river has risen overnight;
now, in the morning, the thaw's brown water
is fleeing away beneath me with a very ill grace.
No simulacrum can last for long in the mirror
of nature. And yet you stand still.
The blood won't abate this morning
either: it's gasping its way,
on the run, through my body as though
there were nowhere to stop any longer.
The far bank is lost in I don't know what.
And there is no ocean far and wide
to throw oneself into. Only extravagant
simulacra in tragical eddies,
gurgling as they founder, go under.

Long-distance call about poetry

Is that you? Yes.
The sentences are fragmenting fast;
words are deserting and settling
down in other languages.
Too many want to have their say
now it's got so cheap.
So lower your voice – the world has
ears. The money's run out. Can you please
spell it? Who is speaking?
Are you still there?

Limestone Quarry

Have you lost something?
I thought
I saw an idea,
when heading for town today,
that used to belong to you
when, together, we used to come
this way, past the quarry
which stalked us with a thousand eyes
as far as the outermost edge of the town.

Two dogs were mating,
toilsomely, though not to be separated
by words, a shuddering oneness
above the abyss concealed
by coltsfoot and by sorrel.

Here I thought
I saw an idea
that, once, had been yours;
it was standing there on the brackish water
down at the bottom of the quarry,
still as a spider.

I threw in a stone and waited
for the echo of childhood –
an echo that turned into circles
out towards the edge which engulfed it
and which engulfed the idea now stalking me
like an extra eye

on my way into town.

This Tree

This tree used, once, to be an idea
planted beneath a serious sky.
They used to say: this tree is a tree
so as not to hurt the idea
that was hiding behind the leaves.

The tree was mentioned with pride, bedecked
with Hope which it then passed on
to the earth or the air, depending.

Some embraced it passionately:
metabolism of sorts
between creaking bark and skin.

This tree was fully occupied,
both as unwearying giver of shade
in times of great heat
and as producer of metaphors.

Look at the tree
on the brow of the hill:
king and citizen, cortex and leaves,
not to forget the root
nor the so supportive earth:
a top-class address of a bygone culture.

People pass by now.
Flapping their arms, they parody
the boughs, shred the shade,
proselytize the earth, as so often:
another semantic revolution.

We call it an accident;
nobody, though, can be brought to book.
Uncouth, we see only pretty sights
where, once, we could make out the natural order.

Thus winter comes.
Rooted to the foot
of the hill, and tiny with cold, with anxiety,
we do our best to give ourselves names:
that tree's eavesdropping, full of suspicion.

Of course

Of course
it would be possible
to call sand
sand again:
to extol
its monotonous grandeur.

Of course
it would be possible
to get in a boat,
to glide across water.

Of course
it would be possible
to cleanse
the memories
leading us up the garden path
of all their grief.   .

Only impatience
saves convention
from a rash end.

Only the vandalization
of paintings
makes us restore them:
overrun, choked
by impatience and guilt,
they hold out their faces
arrogantly to be deciphered.

Of course
it would be possible
to wait for the word
which changes all
(I *have* seen things
that still had no names.).

Of course
it would be possible
to open, again,
the arsenal
of forgotten ideas
to the general public.

The short arm
of Indignation
and
the long arm
of Time.
And both are growing
out of my shoulders
and – as though nothing at all had happened –
are joining hands.

(In mid-sentence,
in mid-fall.)

Of course
it would be possible,
again, to winnow
what's pure from what's not.

Of course
to live would be possible:

of course
of course.

What times are these

Yesterday, in the wood,
a serious talk
with the trees:
if we had our way,
ran their rustling discourse,
there would be no such thing as nature.
What about us, I asked,
alarmed at the prospect of loss,
what on earth would we do without it?
You'd have to make,
out of second, first nature,
answered the trees,
and deal with it
just as you deal with us.
And in the meantime,
the leaves whispered fervently,
we would run wild, wilder than wild,
so that you, as strangers,
could, later, discover us once again.
When they had said this
they vanished for ever.

Footnote

We're coming back to fetch
what remains: pillow; pillow-case; pall;
a drawing which hung unprotected
above the stove: *Hermes, the Guide
of the Dead* who, for the space of four years,
added spice to our meals. God has still
not been born; the clock stays hanging there;
so, in the hall, does the mirror. How
the flat grows and grows, the more it
empties, and how small is Time,
brooding away in the tomb-like rooms.
All is now dark, we've
removed the lamps: everything
passes softly through us. From where
my writing-desk once was,
I try to decipher a note
on the wall: Your Anger is Love.
A footnote in the history
of vanity, still to be written.

Personal Data

Was it a natural death?
Was it a natural life?

Fortune wants to account for its ways
and presents a life:

We see
a biography
buried in words
to the edge and beyond.

We read:
One day
will soon be allowed to be like all others.

Destruction by repetition,
we comment. All voices inside you
will have their whispering say, if you like:

biographies and preconceptions,
a well-turned death
to put the lid on a natural life.

And the eyes, their whites,
for ever blacked out.

(for Hans Bender)

Elegy

Bolzano. A lying in statelessness:
no password exists that could
gain me entry. Some shuffling
gets around like a rumour behind
the mountains; a history, a story
asks the way.

Air, air. Were you waiting
for me who came one day too late?
Your best blue shirt,
your light pair of trousers.
What shall I do with your hand
which can't greet me?

There's snow in your hair,
let me warm you.
Is there a picture of you?
Time has replaced
your body. A stranger,
you're my best friend.

You have to come back
to Germany, Father –
to my side where death
is not spoken about.
You're laughing? Your open mouth
casts suspicion on me. Too late.

How small you are! Though
one grows a little
after death – just as
Death is growing, this moment, in us:
a witness of stainless character
with great clout at court.

A forged passport. Quick;
your life can't be cramped
in obituaries. Two birds are keeping
watch at the border. Beneath
the black body of the clouds,
by stealth, you come back home to us.

Then, at last, earth. At last
the sand of Berlin: up here
you may finally die. You fling Death
like a cloak around your heart of ash
and set yourself free and make no reply
for every answer would be a question.

(for Helmut Otto Krüger)

from
Wiederholungen (1983)

For days and days, an invisible
gardener's been fighting his way through
the shrubs out there in front of my window.
His hands are all I can see
in the feeble sunlight, when the mimosas
part. All predictions,
so vainly guarded, were wrong: I'm
still living. The dust is firmly ensconced
among the loquacious leaves, is sapping
the final green of the year,
the inexhaustible pride that gently
covers both the faces of Hope.

A reason for joy: the sky, at long last,
is open again. Both craftsmen and clockmakers
brood in front of their azure tablet, dating
dillydallying Time. Neither shame nor reserve
interrupts our questioning look
into their long-term research: one hundred
circles, none charmed, none virtuous; and a lacuna
that's gaping, awaiting the jackboot of Power.
Here by the window, my hands clasped behind me,
I'm waiting for the invasion
of night – waiting for it to rupture the frame
which, for weeks now, has dominated, defined me.

The frame once again – the vessel, that is,
within which everything's shaken: stagnation,
but also the frozen heart where worry
finds for itself a different name and emptiness
a religion of strength. And I've got
to spoon up this mess? Yes, you have. One mouthful
for being born, and another for Time
which collared you, and one for the state,
and two for Society for kindly
wiping your mouth clean. Indeed, we all help
to shape this century's physiognomy,
senile and fat, as we are, with our bibs on.

The morning ABC between bed
and writing-table. You're not yet dead,
ergo must practise assiduously;
every day has its problem if every year
has one of its own, every century one,
and so on and so forth, both forwards and backwards.
The problem is seeing today's problem clearly. Today
there's nothing but pure repetition: the din
from the street, in one's head, the sounds
the gardener is making, the windows' drab greyness.
The problem posed by this present day
is Repetition, so get back to bed.

Today in the Pantheon, as I sat down,
downcast, on a bench, set on translating
the daily murders – falteringly – into German, a shaft
of sunlight came through the open dome, transfixing me,
and two birds, strident, screeching, measured the arch with their wings.
Somehow we will survive, in spite of
all the pat maxims that quake with impatience.
Evil endures too. Soon drowned my shout
as I reached the centre, lifted my arms,
and bent back my head between my shoulders;
then ran out, laughing, into the dark.
What a day it was for the beggars!

If you are still unpopular at forty,
you will remain so, to the bitter end.
Confucius said that. The computer ticks:
a familiar doom. Here in Rome,
philosophers come to life in the language
which separates us: we, they say, are ontological
centaurs. Sounds good, and it's true as well.
But, at some point, you will have to decide
where you're going to sleep – for the patrons
who have your feed thrown to you, into your trough,
are dying out. You've got one whole year still,
and this one year will not be diverted.

One could clearly hear the fly on the wall,
so great was the silence. When it had reached
the ceiling, it turned back, then the descent
began without any obvious effort.
No falling, no flying, merely ascent
and descent. Merely work, devoid of knowledge. I sat,
quite still, at the table, my hands resting, still, on my knees,
and learnt this lesson in absolute silence.
One single word could kill the fly, and war
would break out. As it was, though, in silence,
I felt I'd been saved; the mountain of debt
that is cognition amortized itself, in silence.

Is it not fitting
to speak of a 'store
of love'? When all sources
have been destroyed, you anxiously
go back into your heart,
into the counterfeiter's workshop.
Printed feelings,
misprinted time; a dis-
embodied idea excites
the trusty muscle.
The soul keeps on teaching,
but it never repeats itself.

Through repetition, you try to salvage
what is forever abandoning you.
You move one finger, to make a start,
then take four paces in each direction, cast
a glance out of the window, and then get engrossed
in your books. And when, at last, you're exhausted,
you think your way gradually into the history
of exhaustion. But every act
makes a still deeper hole in your modest
hoard of salvaged knowledge. There won't
be much left if you go on like this;
though even a sigh, if deep, is historic.

Owl-light. The indecisive winter,
grey-white, is prone on the city and on
its precipitate prayer: rubbish,
apathy's jetsam, gathers
down in the brownish, boiling river.
Are we in need of a chronicler
for this irreversible strangeness? The guide
enthuses about the sun – which implies
a future of some sort this side
of tears. Truth is human,
and the moment when the hand
decides is a good imitation.

Above all, the uniforms for mourning
and for compassion, the (still to be computed)
demand for defeats, the rising quotas set
for decent dastardliness, R & D
to evolve a technology of cant as an
absolute value – to mention just a few
of our projects. Optimism. We're sorry
to say that our coffers are empty
and, thus, that Life must pick up the bill.
We grant two years discount
and forty years credit. Buying some shares
in this society's well worth while.

Grey; a shadowless period's sending
anaemic light through the lustreless
fabric of the sky. All rules
of time present no longer apply. There's
no acceleration now between the days.
Out of a stone mouth speaks the impatient,
burning desire: that there be evening, light.
Michaelangelo needed four years
for Creation, for Fall,
and for the long, long wait for Redemption;
now it takes twelve to get them cleaned.
Still, the Last Judgement is waiting for colour.

The poem has lost its way. What remains
of its dignity – which we could once still determine
even in history's meanest corners –
looks, amid this affluence, like effluent.
One can like effluent too; it is just that
only traces remain in the vortex of apathy,
only the faintest echo of the vanished poem.
Ought one to search on? That is the question. Is it worthwhile
doing the rounds of the world with a form
to put a couple of words in the right light?
For whether your heart, your embattled heart, will then
be filled with happiness, peace, is far from certain.

Such grim solitude has got its good sides.
Every time that the doorbell rings, you ask yourself –
in all seriousness – if your life
is changing. And thus stay put and let yourself
slip right down into your own four walls.
A coming and going, a coming and going:
a long procession of old acquaintances,
oddly disguised, that you've not seen for ages.
They don't all look like you but they all have
some tic you recognize right from the start.
A silent nod or two, every now and then a gesture.
Everyone grimly clings to their privacy down in the south too.

A vigil for the dead. Turned to the wall;
my breath takes me with it
into the picture in which distant cataracts
rinse out your head.
All is deciphered, nothing is known;
my knowledge is not great enough
for me to be near you. Nothing
is framed by form, my hand's
like Tantalus'. Only, below,
the river – whose waters are
growing calmer – releases pictures
and bones which don't match.

Rain, rain, rain. Its placid whispering
tempers nature's pathos-laden prophecy.
Here in this world of liberties, where one person
wants to go places, where another does not
because, in his view, it no longer pays,
you fervently wish you were back in the loam
of your birthplace: nothing makes better sense
than criticizing Repetition in such foul weather.
The Roman she-wolf still has
many free teats to which you can cling –
resigned, and afraid that your memories
are being washed out of your heart of ash.

He who came out of the 'underground'
or in from 'cold' history,
the thoroughly disaccustomed man –
who scoffs at the paper,
ensures that all the pictures are crooked,
who drinks up my wine
and thinks he is 'loaded' –
proposes to me
that we go to the graveyard today
and wait there *until the*
crawling populus follows;
why, he refuses to say.

Behind the heads of the warriors
ruins, behind these the sea.
One man, as tall as I am, stepped
right out of the picture,
three hundred years back.
How are things? He's wearing a species
of gymshoe, but is making
no headway. How lucky for me
to have a hard pencil
with which to escape
across the white sea. He, though, remains,
and only briefly loosens his helmet.

I know exactly where you are:
your steps in my head,
which crush the moment underfoot,
are slowly, unhurriedly, clattering back,
back to the unattainable day.
Letters, telephone-calls, a visit
to Gramsci's grave: all of the graves
return my greeting, unheedingly,
with sodden hearts. One must be allowed
to live without being happy, without
having roots in these graves
which betray the moment.

Christmas. A haughty poem is writing
itself across the hills of
Montefollonico: two pines,
a break, one cypress, one pine etc. etc.
GOD commands to be written in
upper-case letters; the rest,
in this Second Age of Prose,
is mighty hard to decipher. The willing wind too
is only a philologian *manqué*.
If we were down there pushing up daisies,
the text on the hillside
would annotate itself in a trice.

Still too little at home behind
the foolish mask of Happiness: your look
will not acclimatize. A gingko tree
in the park of the Villa Borghese; a ball
that bounces, crimson, over the parapet;
lovers fiercely grilling each other,
locked in cold cars in front of the ruins.
The essence of these paper-thin days
invariably fades in unfaithful books.
Only because we wish to be are we
weary of praising: in Night's thin filter,
pessimists manage to save their bacon.

Flocks of birds up above the city.
Screeching, in geometrical circles,
they're swimming in the
old silver of the last day
of the year – and are seeing something
that keeps on eluding us, there in the
unprotected centre of the city.
I don't go to look. To disguise
my dreams, I sit and wait
at my desk. For if someone
should wish to make contact,
he really should find me hard at work.

Hopelessly late. Outside
the new year's already rampant, and
inside, as so often today,
thoughts of the old year dominate.
One's pullover smells of cold smoke
and of a decision not made.
Take comfort: every poem arrives
too late, even though its every word
adds to the house behind whose window
you're now appearing. Take comfort: this window
could not be opened, even though the house were falling
apart in front of your very eyes.

At stake is not the apex
of the pyramid, rather its base,
the hierarchy's starting-point. At stake,
if you like: the imprisoned child
which does not know the way,
no, worse, which does not know
there is a way, in its cubby-hole –
as high as the bottom freestone, as low.
How can it – how could it – describe a way
when it is, quite literally, losing its life?
Thus, it is left locked up in its gaol
while, at the apex, the Meaning appears.

He cuts a fine figure,
standing there so motionless,
so inscrutably open
to all the fortuities of Night.
No debauch could entice him
to sell short the heritage of the eyes.
He sees. Indeed, he personifies sight.
He stands there like a ruin
that time can no longer harm,
just like a fiction that suddenly froze
in my field of vision, right
in front of my window, staring hard at me.

Someone is painting. Someone is writing. Someone
is sitting at the piano, expectantly,
by an open window. The 'End of Art'
is somehow present, now here, now there
in the corner amidst the assorted rubbish,
disguised as a prompter: thus come into being
a colourful flask here, and there the Conquest of the Moon,
and in the middle a little piece of piano-music
already detached from what was the intention that's
left as a husk: 'There is Necessity, there is
God': and, whilst we're exchanging sheepish looks,
Redemption comes in the form of thin rain.

(for Erich Heller)

When his dreams had outwitted him,
he'd swim, in the small hours, in the small moat
surrounding his villa, against the clock
which counted his hours in wintertime too.
All can be copied; the shortest quotation
is, always has been, the world which he saw
on his three expeditions. One crocodile,
four caryatids and two sileni,
and looks and stones – that's all that there was
on the scrolls in the courts of the libraries.
For four years the emperor lived in his copy
of the world; and then the empire went to the cats.

Via two swivelling bridges, the emperor
reached the heart, returning by water
to the centre. Here he then mused
on the narrowing bridges
between mythology, prophecy
and on those between centre and outermost rim.
A look was to help him,
a look sent through forty Ionic pillars:
there in the west, where the sun was once again going down,
there the herb that cures delusion had to be growing.
Or may one envisage cosmic destruction
in order to salvage Paradise?

This paradise was the vanishing-point;
Oblivion was practised there in strict
seclusion. All tricks of thinking – thought
through with the sword – found a ready brain
outside the door; the emperor, however,
put his ear against the stone mouth
and had all wishes recounted to him
from the end of the world until its beginning.
The jagged profile of experience
(river, mountain and hut, but also the path to the sea)
had to round itself off in a sphere that he wished
to be buried smack at the vanishing-point.

The fire-brigade's blue light keeps leaping
across the street outside my window,
every day, several times a day. The city,
it seems, must burn in circles round my house
(the sky is completely cloudless, the Tiber
gurgling nonchalantly in its bed).
The bucket sloshes from hand to hand,
and loses water outside my window
before it gets to the nearby fire.
Look how quickly everyone's running!
Frozen in a childhood pose,
I stand at the window, awaiting the blaze.

All of a sudden, the sky begins
to listen to reason, and nobody knows:
could this be some sort of answer to
the steady flow of investment or else
a paying-back in the same
currency? At any rate,
it bodes no good.
The weathermen are slow to react,
then issue new coins
with surprising reliefs:
above outstretched hands curves
the other, the different, balance-sheet.

But it could happen: the book
could get opened again, could get laid
on its spine once again by a gust of wind
that came into being when the book was banged
shut, long ago; that gobbled
its way through history, a rotter;
and suddenly, now, in the darkness,
returns. It could well be
that a page is still blank
and offers itself: yellowed already,
crumbly, but longing for one last
line: what would you write?

The innocence or primal virtue
of reading is a last social mystification,
akin to the sexual innocence of childhood,
or of womanhood. Reading, when active,
and interesting, is not less aggressive
than sexual desire, or than social ambition,
or professional drive. On the other hand,
I know a woman who makes a good living
from writing love-poems: her readers assume
it has all been 'felt'. Those pangs in the chest,
those twinges and stabs, that high-powered moaning:
there's no way she could have got *all* that from books.

It isn't that which drives you on,
it is far more. It's not the shadow
cast on the wall, outstripping you,
nor the long-lost idea that still —
in the form of a copy — oppresses you.
It is far more. It ought to be more
than father and mother and child, more too
than the weak light which cannot point to a source.
It might be more still, more than all
delusions, more than the drop,
the wave, the water and the ocean.
More than the sum of Repetition.

When, thus, the text seeks us
and not vice versa (H. Bloom),
when we have to open ourselves so it doesn't
miss us, the time for waiting
has come, i.e. waiting until the paper
turns black in front of your eyes,
without paying heed to the
subtle promptings of Worry and Fear,
the whisperings of the Evil Sisters
who'd like to conceal themselves deep in the text
to appear as a poem,
white, on black paper.

Definitive. A word that, for days,
has been hounding me.
When I try to escape,
it bars my way till
I mouth it, but still:
the walk comes to grief.
At table — tasteless —
it sits in the food;
when I'm reading, it stains
the characters red.
Only now, as I break its back de-
finitively, does it throw in the sponge.

Fama est. The rumour is ticking
away in the walls; and cracks
are appearing. Near letter-boxes,
posing as postman, stands the informer,
smiling and nodding in my direction.
Yesterday, it was Dante still;
today, I have to contribute at last
to Domestic Peace.
But in what coin if the hard
Dantesque currency's not legal tender?
There's no need to hear any evidence:
the sentence was, after all, passed long ago.

The rumour lives on, badly needed,
besought, by those who are writing
the history of baseness.
How futile, dear Mrs Lonelyhearts,
were your letters if now
unslept-in beds are writing
their memoirs? But such art will last
as long as there's art
that hates itself. How thankful I am
to give the cat food!
She'll soon have a litter, and then
there'll be life in this place once again.

As in a fairy-tale, as abruptly,
the questions vanished.
Only soft, smooth faces were bending down
over my window, here and there
some splashes of colour, but nothing wild,
and certainly no religion
one simply had to stand up for.
Had there been a lake nearby,
we could have gone swimming
and Truth would have slipped
between our wet hands,
as in summer, as in a fairy-tale.

It's not that I expected something –
expecting all, I expected nothing –
certainly not this manner of greeting,
not this white breath
which refused to dissolve,
and not these white letters
which stopped up my mouth.
Why pretend to be a father
when I've no child?
And why look kindly at that old girl
when she goes and spills the milk and that man
over there begins to laugh up his sleeve?

This palace here administers
the hunger of another world.
The king's advancing on the pawns –
quite coolly. Check!
Look how icy the queen is looking!
Will she get as far as the castle?
Telling against her: both the perspective
and her fallow dignity.
I'd like to join in, the situation
is really not hopeless. Oh yes it is:
the pawns are turning the tables on them,
the pawns have chubby little red cheeks.

Let us now work, that is:
pray. The rosary's
beads, which are made of blood,
flow gently through the knowing hand.
It's you
because you don't exist.
(Already you hear
the booming clattering of the steps
going backwards:
in the city's wings.)
The centre is bleeding,
the filthy periphery's bleeding to death.

A patient reminiscence
goes with you through the wood:
Pine, olive, box and myrtle,
laurel, chestnut, scrub oak.
Fed
into the embracing machine
as the earth lies in the soft arms
of the atmosphere: the base
has worn thin, the world's
coming through.
Clean-shaven, hunchbacked hills
grow over the reminiscence.

You can't be a guest here any longer –
the chairs are all taken. And it is late;
the interpretations are lying like crumbs
there on the table, the text has been broken.
You'd like to explain to them why you are here,
but everyone raises their hands: we know,
we know, all is known.
You're still tolerated, your back
to the wall, a listening-post.
What are poems about? The city
is stiff with posters: È ora
di dire basta. Yes, it *is* high time.

from
Stimmen (1983)

Straight on, let yourself be driven, the voice
powers the wheel. At the end of the path:
a house, go on, let yourself in, the voice
will show you your room. If you're moved
to ask who is speaking, let well alone, the voice
knows no answer. Go to sleep.

Freshly felled trees, look,
barring the path; the wood is releasing
its voices from the undergrowth –
narrated suffering, leaf by leaf.
What was long silent inside you finds
language; an unhoped-for wind
takes each of your words along with it.

Voices coming from both sides. I have to repeat
each one of these words that is guarding
my sleep (the busy frontier between me
and me), protecting the one man from
the other. In times of peace,
it's easy enough to reach the place
where one man, consumed by his death-wish, is speaking
and where the other is wordlessly showing his
empty hands. But now it is war-time.
Lined up in the same rank: I and I,
word against word, and neither knows
to whom this word belongs with which we,
empty of words, are fighting each other.
O yes and the voice-researchers' whispers
ensure that we sleep through every victory.

Near Haag. The lost, shy faces of sheep
that are straining to listen. The realm of remembrance
is growing bigger, the ratio changes radically:
an outsize insect creeping backwards
with minute feelers, blind. The present
must be here somewhere in this field;
one only has to connect up the lines
between the molehills, and then its face
will at once appear. If only that dog would not keep on
running around that circle! If only a word were uttered, at last.
The shepherd, however, has been struck dumb
and I have no ripping yarn to tell either.

Bright spots on the forest floor, too late
for this time of day. A water clock ticks,
and – in the space between two falling drops – Memory
triumphs. The tongues are already retiring
beneath the raspberries. An old paper sports
a photo of Stalin with eyes that are moist.
The voice, in the end, grows quieter, and Time
stretches out between the words. Animals' bones
and feathers line the path till it ends.

How small we become
beneath this voice
which belongs to a bird
only slightly above us.
Small
like a monosyllabic word
behind the looming wall of rain
which, booming, hides you.

Nothing is vouched for. Yet when,
too weary to speak, we crossed
the voice which, late in the evening,
slowly follows remembrance,
we saw a small paper ship
that was pluckily weaving its way
through the delta of words.
Nothing is vouched for. Yet when,
too weary to look, we traversed
remembrance which, on such days,
had torpidly left our hearts,
we quite distinctly heard someone whisper:
I am, I am, I am.
Nothing is vouched for. Yet when,
too weary to listen, we found
our way home one night,
the voice was already there and spoke
out of us: babbling, as though to small children.

Lost votes, lost voices. Dance of the gestures
whenever the Answer won't multiply:
before you the mountains, bright in the foehn,
the lake (which is green for all insiders),
the stable forest there to the south. Assume
the interpretation includes you: is the place
from which, with one look, you are getting the picture
to speak still part of the picture in question
or is it outside it?
You long to go home. You look at
your imprint on the meadow,
the different green that preserves your body
here, for an instant.
You've got to go. At the picture's
emergency exit, grasses
choke your voice when you answer the question
'What is Life?': 'I cannot interpret;
I see the interpretation includes me.'

Repeat your words
courageously in the hideout
of language (in front of the entrance
alien voices are keeping a whispering look-out
for you). When evening brings you
into the world (when the other
voices dissolve into silence), venture
out without any qualms:
then, from the silence, word by word,
you'll recover the world.

The Voice of the Bird

1

Whoever still doubts should
take a good look at the tremulous bird
above the lake. It can soar or swoop
but will never brush the water's
surface. It could fly back
along the track of the thread one can't see
which is fastened there within the horizon.

2

That is the way that it measures time. Its shadow
passes tremulously across your body,
a moving target marking the spot
where you're at your most mortal.
Lying there, waiting, in your boat,
your eyes stare up into heaven until
the shadow finally brushes your face.

3

The sight of the bird revives dreams
you believed were long forgotten,
scenes of separation that rise from
out of the depths and make the boat roll.
The world now forces you out of the shadow
of the bird and drives you off course into merry
hell – where there's no point at all in measuring time.

4

The voice of the bird gets fainter,
but the image remains: for all who still
doubt.

Above the slope...

Above the slope
are birds, treading air;
the lost body's scarcely
touched by their calls.
Even before their names,
I knew their
land-eating look.
I think my way into you
like a bird.
And the wind that is
blasting, blasting your face
bears your voice backwards,
clearing the sky, up
above the slope.

from
Die Dronte (1985)

Alive as a Dodo

1

No eggs, no integuments.
Only a head exists and two feet,
four-toed for scratching,
which came into contact with
tuff, basalt lava,
ash and slag,
and carried a body
that seems lost for ever.

2

Dodo, dudu, didus ineptus:
this creature took refuge
in a glass-case in the
Senckenberg Museum in Frankfurt.
What we see
might well be Truth:
dusty grey down
which quivers at every single heartbeat.

3

If we go back far,
the border gets porous:
bird-calls passing from here to beyond,
and, after the fire,
a low human voice
as the wind desired:
you have to decide.

4

The following centuries
were ours: pictures of patience,
we sat there under the dusty glass,
naked exhibits, head and foot,
direction and steering.
What we discovered disappeared
like the plans of the cosmos.
And we discovered a good, good deal.

5

Like a text
which effaces itself;
like a dark movement
beneath a night sky;
like the final day above water.
No one has ever seen
this bird since 1620.

6

Città del Sole; thirty years' war;
On the Three Lives of Man;
nutritional problems.
The dodo gets silenced
by history: she could
not fly. Only her name
was rescued from her future foes,
from Time and Death;
along with a head and two feet.

7

(A painting depicting the bird
is said to hang in Berlin
but no one recalls it;
several old studies
mention that the flesh is bitter.)

8

The seas have been measured
and space depleted
and longing long ground
right down to nothing
by ruthless cognition.
Then the Gods became visible
and withdrew
for ever.

9
The dodo is the bird of love:
she dreams up a body and mighty wings
for herself and, at once,
she's sitting – and speaking –
on my shoulder.

10
We do not know
what is really ours.
A wingbeat, a picture
drawn from nature in an old book.
A word
sealed in stone,
and the stone in the layer of red clay
down underneath the dust.

11
This bird keeps Memory
alive; she sees
what, for us, is fading fast,
wrapped in a hope
which only comes to fruition once.

12
The whole of space
is abuzz with this hope;
there's no more to be said.

A conversation while it rains

Just as the rain is furiously beating
away at the earth and a headstrong wind
is doing its damnedest to fuse with the house
in which we are sitting, so too ideas
have done no more than scratch the world's surface,
have not sunk in. The changes, if any,   ·

cannot be gauged, at most on a time-scale
on which we humans have no place.
No niche will be reserved for us,
for our idea of harmony;
reconciling breath and flight
will prove quite futile. All will remain

the way it is, except without us.
Maybe our forms will therefore turn out
to be the last ones, although the outside
will give away nothing about the content: all the same,
there will still be rhythm, and breaks in rhythm,
and frozen screams. Scratching the surface,

not sinking in. Perhaps it is wrong,
he mumbled on, to make a distinction
between a wish and its fulfilment. Nevertheless,
such a distinction means that we needn't
clap our hands at our own execution.
That's at least something. Scratching the surface,

not sinking in. The rain is splashing
down from the roof onto the gravel
down on the forecourt, forming puddles
for the birds which drink to the water –
wild pigeons are celebrating the Rain-Feast.
Snarled up inside ourselves, we drink too,

listening to the haggard voices,
whispering, questioning, round the house,
and watching the various changes, watching
what's done and what's not done (one can't tell the difference).
Scratching the surface, not sinking in ever.
And there behind the grey sheet of rain:

a pallid glimmer, as though from a cloud
with the sun inside it, a sun which it aches
to put out with a hug.

From the cycle *Roman Winter*

The gardener is building a brave new wall
with stones that are old. Old stones, he exclaims
in a fit of pride: nothing goes to waste in this world.
His hands should certainly know. I return
to the writing-table, to empty
paper: 'Nothing goes to waste', writes
my hand, which I thought that I knew,
'in this world'. I run out into the open –
circuitously, through many doors – and squeeze
the gardener's hand. We talk for a good long time
about the weather: the day has been saved.
Proudly, with dirty hands, I return.

An architect is dead drunk – it happens.
With shaky hands, he draws a villa
on to the air: the poet's villa.
Capacious rooms that open onto the ancient world.
Then he describes the world (its downfall),
and pulls down the villa with drunken words.
Relishing this, he pours himself more.
One can't imagine the villa without this world, and thus
it must be destroyed when this gets destroyed.
What of the poet? I ask. Does he get
away to herald the downfall of both?
Eh? What poet? he asks, and nods off.

I know what I wanted to say to you last time
we talked, when words failed me: there is such a thing
as a sanguine coward who, turning tail,
reveals himself to the world as a weakling:
Things will come right (although he is looking
straight at the sensitive plants that are shining
luridly in the dusk). But there is also another
type of sanguinity, powerless and strong:
the beggar Repetition. And thus
the trembling of your hand, which touches his hand,
lives on. And, there behind him, you spot
in the wall a slight chink which soothes you.

Disarmed: I've made a
confession. Now your work begins –
checking, assessing, rejecting,
word by word. Inspecting,
armed with a scholar's inquisitiveness,
a sentence that's difficult to decipher.
Just be patient: the criminal always
returns to the scene of the crime, then it's easy.
The archives are blank, the books
refuse to pass commentary,
the body steals away while
we speak. The confession expires.

All the same, I stick to my guns – confessing
that the 'crime' will follow. It is the sentence
after which everything falls into place;
we are speaking of Life. It's not vanity,
cowardice, nor the need to say something,
anything, so as to break an appalling
silence that's got me to speak. A man who is stealing
God's days, God's minutes, is watching the phone;
the windows are barred; I see the street
through a haze of barbed-wire. Something's
exposed; and I know how foolish
it is to substitute love for a void.

The 'man without spot' is in town again –
I saw him today in the Piazza del populo,
barefoot in sandals: with hands raised to bless,
he vehemently laid into the church.
He that hateth his life in this world
shall keep it, unto life eternal.
Little Korean nuns were agog;
Indian Christians; a towering black,
mythically tall, with eyes like flames,
with a black sword quivering in his mouth,
who was wearing a bloody cloak and had diadems
on his head; and I too of course.

It isn't easy to enter a church after that. Thank
goodness: a beggar is sitting on the wet steps
of S. Maria del Popolo, with running sores
all down his dirt-caked legs, stretching out
a talon-like hand to you. You pay. His hair is short
and black and stubbly like that of the man
in Caravaggio's painting, who has
to help to carry St Peter's cross. His woollen shirt
has ridden up, his breeches are green.
…in hoc signo vinces? I wouldn't ever wish to be saved
beneath that sign…What an art of transformation! Electric
candles light up his filthy soles.

Painting as a school of dread: with a foot
on the head of the snake, the child
is watching the writhing body. Words
well up within it, which it relays
to the ear of Power. The painter never
grew up, so they say; his hidden motives
stay buried in darkness: his life's sign-language
has not been deciphered even now.
Why did he become a painter? Out of despair?
Unlikely. Happiness, so they taught him,
has to be bought with Suffering. Nothing
the eye can size up, but it trips off the tongue.

Follow me! But why me? asks M
who is, whose left hand is, still playing with coins;
I'm winning! In his dark pupils, however,
intensely promoted by the light,
a different world's thriving. There's not much left
in store for him; if we shift our gaze,
the hangman is looming up above him,
figura serpentinata, a sword –
unsheathed – in his fist. In the background, the painter
is watching and knows that that's how he too
will, one day, end up. The deed, however, is still covered up
by the soot of the candles that stand on the altar.

He had no disciples, no assistants,
just imitators. Stones, plants, herbs,
the strain in the muscle of an assassin,
the lurid gleam in the eye of a cow
and, again and again, brows prodigiously knitted;
everything he developed himself
in the magic triangle of his painting.
When painting his allegory Love Triumphant
over Art, he painted the End of Painting too:
Nature had given him masters enough.
The police have a file, a meticulous file,
on his boundless passion.

He hurled a bowl of fruit at the head
of a waiter in the Albergo del Moro;
later, he slayed his fellow-painter Tommasoni;
in between times, he painted Truth – so absolutely
we have to turn away in shame.
Numerous paintings: removed
or cleaned up. But the son of a mason
simply would not be brushed off. Only once
did he paint an artificial source of light
(a torch), and otherwise only natural,
supernatural light. To bring out
the Seven Works of Charity, to make them shine.

Just one example: Cimon puts his ageing head
between the bars and Pero, his daughter, clandestinely
gives him her breast. She lives next door;
as a Dead Mary we see her again,
her corpse all bloated, or else as Mary
with hair done up, her chapped hands red
with continual washing. The saints, as well,
are familiar, even Christ (Doubting Thomas
is thrusting his filthy fingers into Jesus's wound).
Later, all prop up the bar at Gino's,
smoking and chatting and drinking their coffee,
until they are needed again as models.

He wanted to be sheer eye, a single libidinous eye
his whole gaunt body. When they discovered him,
dead, at Porto Ercole, on the beach, they found
he'd worked his face into the sand, in shame, because
he'd seen himself entirely at last
in his killers. Brother Killer, I see
myself through the slits of your screwed-up eyes.
These brutes were the first to recognize
the origin of the light whose source
has been sought for so long. Enlightened Caravaggio,
with sand in your wide-open eyes: all things
you wanted to see, yourself too as victim.

Does the image I make of you
resemble the image you make of me?
If so, it would be self-criticism
to criticize one another: I love you
in your split seconds of indecision.
Quickly a walk, an upright eyeing-
up of the natives: what do they make of
you, an upright German who gapes,
so openly, at them? Go back now, phone:
of course you're not there. I let it ring
until your image appears, and then ask:
What do you think, when thinking of me, about yourself?

Anamorphosis

We know this look, the look of the forger,
staring rigidly into the cold.
We know this hand that enjoins
silence on us: we're bound
not to tell of the things that we've seen.
We make off, and get scaled down
by the surface – he stares as we shrink.

A pause; a lost echo;
his shadow catches us up just
short of the edge of the picture
where animals cringe beneath bushes,
quaking. We are not we
when we turn round, once again, to look back,
and he is not he any longer: his body

a sombre landscape, his hand
a star that is shedding kind light on this
wrong wrought by nature: a small heap of ashes;
a couple of bones; some wind, broken-winded,
that's toying listlessly with the remains.
A story that interrupts itself:
its end a beginning.

Palpitations

It is the simple, the straight-
forward things that keep us from sleeping:
a palpitation,
a hand seized hold of,
a looking around in black amazement.
Not the muddled play of one's thoughts,
not the eccentric ruminations,
not the fantastical masque
of Truth.
It is the great footprint
which unexpectedly shows us the way,
half commanding, half blessing;
and, with hearts pounding,
we stumble through sleep.

Domestic Slaughtering

1
The bothered look
that encounters itself:
inscribed on the body
whose fleeting warmth
is heating the stones.
The centre
is filled with Death,
with all photos
that give birth to Death.

2
The dead beast
is washed:
the writing effaced
in front of our eyes.
What does not speak
doubles up, and fits
into the everyday archive of victims.
You too: a victim,
a look-victim, copied.

3
All things
have their place
(it is written);
and we are watching
them seeking their place
in the emptying
picture.
You are the butcher,
the slaughterer,
and I am the meatman,
open-eyed.

4
A pig, a sow,
a piglet or wild sow
is now being slaughtered.
They thought you were alien,
did you in too.
We slaughter in pictures
from nature, from life.
Only much later
does language strike us,
only much later,
on the placards of Dread,
do we read: the shriek.

5
The blood slops
across the visual threshold,
the corse
becomes us: we hear ourselves
heartily smacking our lips.

Princeton, N.J.

Sometime or other, you make yourself felt
(like the wind in the yard)
between two breaths,
and then, for a long time, I sit
by the shore – indolent, glad
to know that there is a place on the map
that's no longer snow-bound.
And I imagine
a plain, simple sky,
both body and shadow,
gently laid across the flat land,
across the house that accommodates you,
across the voice that is speaking you too.

The thaw's set in here –
the snow which eavesdropped on the town,
for such a long time, sets another town free.
When the light starts to burn in the orange-tree,
when the mad birds, right at the top of their voices,
count the hours and when I can't see
myself any more in the dusty window,
then I'm all patience and turn the pages
of atlases and ancient books
that picture sorrow so patiently.

And, sometime or other, I fall asleep,
my finger on a distant place
on a map that shows another world
that is like our own.
And, just as I do, the sun rises there.

An old story I

There in a puddle, after the deluge,
I saw the world. There were sandstone houses,
blue-roofed, with withering weeds
on the walls, and scudding clouds,
lazily lounging around in the depths,
and narrow roads, broken-open, yawning,
effortlessly holding the sky
and the little left over: the wishes
which shot through the surface
of this world like bright showers. I saw
the wind which was reaping the woods
with its trusty scythe, and saw Time too,
concealed in the hollowness of a grotto,
just like a fish that one notices only
when, with the slightest flick of a fin,
it vanishes. All this I saw,
and it pleased me not to see
the country that should have been mirrored
there in the puddle, after the deluge.

On Insomnia

Already the drag-marks of the phenomena
Yesterday, breathing heavily, tugged
into the waking-room have been removed:
a letter, a phone-call, a wrong decision
and, if I'm right, a right one too.

Yesterday itself has vanished
into Tomorrow, leaving no trace – if the black space
which borders on the dark waking-room
is really the future. I am uncertain:
the letter, at any rate, gleams like a star,

abstract, purged of all signification.
The phone-call is a precious object
imperceptibly moving: being-on-the-move
as stasis in a world without time.
The wrong decision is a window,

painted, bright, into the dark space,
behind which the sun keeps rising and setting
as though in a fairground stall; the right one
a rosemary shrub that a fox cub
is carrying in its mouth. And Death's in the dark

as to who, with closed eyes, is staring at him.
He's designing a sleep which is a degenerate
form of waking, a busy, bustling kind of seclusion;
planning a deprivation that starts an incurable craving
for a world which is near, which is quite beyond reach.

A Letter from Rome

1

On one of the very few bright mornings
in February, thick red sand dust lay
on the window-sills, doubtless
from Africa, maybe Tunisia,
dropped here in Rome by a
sensitive wind. A rare occurrence
in February which I wanted to mark.
I started to write on the three window-sills
in the way one writes with a finger
on sand: a soft calligraphy
full of round forms that – some time or other –
will be destroyed by some gentle rain.

2

Some time or other. It was a poem
about the small stretch of desert within us,
about the sand which, as long as we live,
we count in our roaming hope
for knowledge, about the countless imitations,
about the uncountable repetitions.
The last line ran: My anguish
ceased, my cares blew away.
My index-finger was burning but I
felt no pain: the text
had been written and no gentle rain
would ever be able to blot it out.

3

And, as you know, it rained a good deal
this February, here in this world
of crumbling stone which put
the text to the test. And us too.
The sky: a corrupt, an impure source.
Nothing, however, could get me to doubt
the connection existing between the red sand,
that had flown across the benighted sea,
and the carefully copying hand
that, against the run of experience, ordered that sand.
Beaches thus come into being on which
we peacefully sit, on to which we're cast up.

A Lecture

1

I think you must have made some mistake:
for I was not up there on the rostrum at all,
substantiating 'properly-founded
moral judgements'. I was just one
of the audience, sitting between an old lady
for whom 'good' and 'bad' did not need to be
substantiated, and a young blonde
who sighed the whole time and kept
making notes I could not decipher.

2

It struck me as strange that all
moral judgements date so quickly;
not that this bothered the lecturer,
who battens on it. As he was trying
to differentiate 'right needs' from 'wrong' ones,
I really couldn't help thinking of you:
'Everyone ought to do what he thinks
is right, even though it proves to be wrong.'
Was, I wonder, the way we behaved
objectively right or wrong? The philosopher's
answer is that there can be no answer,
for reasons that have to do
with linguistic analysis.

3

After the lecture, I went to a bar
and drank your health in gin
and tonic. There isn't, of course,
a Higher World which assigns, beams down,
our 'moral judgements' to us; there's merely
the humdrum rut of history
in which they somehow evolved, in which
they now have somehow withered away.
All that remains are moral feelings,
a sort of philosophical pittance.
A friend in America recently wrote
that all he now wants to do is describe
the wagging of the tail of his dog; he can
no longer picture a different type of literature.

4
How glad I was to be home again,
within my alien four walls. For hours on end,
I rearranged the books, weeded out
a lot that had been like bibles to me –
but no new order, no really new order, came of it.
I sense what is wrong, I think that I know
what's unreasonable, I've done all I can
to remember all the 'right' tenets and precepts.
It's just: they refused to be remembered.
In a dream, I did something that was, at once,
both moral, reasonable and right;
you were involved. It was, by the way,
a nightmare I woke from drowning in sweat.

One Woman, One Lady

1

She makes some coffee.
Back in the room, she asks:
milk? Then fetches some.
Back in the room, she asks:
sugar? Then fetches some.
She herself takes milk and sugar.
She chain-smokes,
has a hacking cough.
Her first husband died, in '44,
at the hands of the Germans.

2

A left-wing independent,
she sits (three times
a week) in Parliament.
It's just round the corner.
For her, the premier
is a fixed-term
bandit. You can't
imagine what lies fly about in that place.

3

In her apartment,
in a palazzo in the centre,
it's bitterly cold and utterly quiet;
books and paintings. Where may I
put my overcoat?
The baker's boy
has moved to the country. Many, she says,
are sick of Rome. She also knows
what the butcher's kids
are up to. She knows everything.
She does not brag. She sadly says:
the family has been blotted out.

4

The bookshops in Rome
are being displaced by
shoeshops; those who are on the dole,
she says, do not read books very often. Are things
any different with you? She is wearing
an old, dark jersey;
her hair is short and iron-grey.

5

When I talk about her books,
she shyly smiles. Childhood has nothing
to do with innocence. *Tutti i nostri ieri*. Franz,
the Jew, has no real-life counterpart.
We were a large, large family.

6

It's getting harder and harder
to write.

7

I'd like to have you as an
opponent, I say. She laughs and
smooths her black skirt straight. Do you know
the ruses of Power?
She's writing no novels at the moment
since there are other pressing problems –
the Pope, for instance.

8

Arrivederla, Signora Ginzburg.
She lives on the 5th floor;
a palace does not boast a lift.

Ernst Meister in memoriam

In things
the eyes, Ernst,
prior to language.
Wherever you are
you return:
stone, threshold, house
are watching you closely.
Therefore, Ernst,
you remain alive,
always in view.

Guided Tour of a well-known house

You cannot bring yourself to see the nursery
because it would remind you of your own;
nor do you wish to see the unthankful cellars,
which are the same as all unthankful cellars,
nor the grey gloaming in the unused kitchens,
the vestibules and drawing-rooms,
the look-constricting corridors
teeming with warning-signs and little stories
scrawled on the walls,
in blood, by roving relatives.
You have to give the sacred rooms a miss,
in which the occupants learnt the art of thinking;
the legendary rooms too, for that matter,
which are now empty, reek of emptiness.
The torture-chambers merit not one glimpse,
nor do the lofts, the quite insatiable lofts.
You pass the whispering-galleries by,
and also give a wide berth to each door
behind which Memory is working,
floor by floor.
The house is shedding history.
You sink down on the lowest step,
putting your weary feet upon the threshold,
on to the threshold which was once God-fearing,
then get them to describe to you
the one room that a look has never ravaged.

from
Zoo (1986)

Leopardi and the Snail

A snail is crawling across the terrace,
a slimy gastropod safely escaped from the
unquiet garden. Dainty and lithe and corneous,
she is vacuum-cleaning, directed by
a magnet underneath the tiles. With head held high,
this sacred animal, hurtfully dignified, starts to cross
the ants' thoroughfare where business is booming
and burdens change backs till one's gaze is confounded.
One of the sisters of Sisyphus,
who toils on the flat, a natural foe
of Repetition.
The centre is reached, as quietly as though
the shell of the world – shot through with imperceptible
cracks – must not be shaken.
Don't turn your thoughts to Time, Happiness;
unless we are tragic, we can't be immortal.
But how can one bring home the fact that the world
would be out of joint without this snail which has
now completed the white minute hand of her cosmic clock?
Why on earth, says Leopardi, should we have been born
except to see how happy we would have been
not to have been?

Walk with a Blind Man

The sun has got stuck in the mist; there behind
the wood, white type, some smoke is rising,
wisps like miserable galley proofs, and the cold is providing
the punctuation: today the sad beauty
of early children's books is abroad.
Brighter than white, can you still remember?
The earth is thin, like an ancient coin,
its profile worn down. He wants to go on,
get smaller as the century ends,
then vanish somewhere in birchy radiance.
Visually lazy, image-weary, I'd like to remain
in the hollow there on the slope, to stare
at the sky which no longer believes its eye.
He, though, is keen to continue, quite deaf
to the death of the tiny dumb beasts underfoot,
blind to the night. He says: in this way,
I am helping to do your seeing while you are doing mine.

Crickets

Keep it up, onwards,
as long as Reality
says you are right.
Keep it up, onwards,
with small steps backwards,
so small that they painlessly
fit in between two words, in between
two tortured man's screams.
The script – illegible
even before the book falls apart.
On the inside of grief:
the animals' score.
Crickets, written in blood.

Retort

Don't say that Death
is impartial, indifferent;
it makes its selection most scrupulously.
Today it requires a head
in which arcana are sleeping
like slothful old cats.
Yesterday it chose a fool
who commended detours: something
gratuitous must, he said, happen
or else we will never get closer
to Love. What of tomorrow?
It is the vicarious voice
that replies,
the alien tongue, invariably –
he who selects or rejects
leaves instructions that he is not in.
Today the dog from next door
died too, which used to yap
as though it were trying to scare away God.

Analogy

Some mistake? Where nothing looks
like itself any more, your thirst
for analogies seems pretty suspect. Leave things
as they are – they only compare with themselves.
When dust gets kicked up, then dust gets kicked up.
Just wait until it has settled again, then
dust has settled again. Do not ask
how it has settled again: that is no
concern of yours. Too much comparing
soon has you sitting at Hatred's feet. First thing,
when your face is, again, free of lather,
you look like yourself, that's the end of the matter.
Unless you're altogether mistaken.

Walk with a Philosopher

What's *not* banal? Please don't get me wrong:
politics, also ideas... at the end of time,
and the end is really in sight, after all,
what's not banal? Seductiveness, charm
are the merest dead letters; at the end of time,
the will to speak has been finally broken.
Please don't invoke Experience –
one really shouldn't, I feel, really shouldn't.
Against the background of such indifference,
you can't expect answers from *écriture*.
There, by the roadside, the corpse
of a cat, its mouth wide-, wide-open,
its bloodstained fur matted. One has to
let dead time live, he opines,
that is the only chance that we have:
one's got to react appropriately.
And the Apocalypse? Well, the thing is that
passions too get administered.
And, don't forget, the Apocalypse
is only the O of a cat's open mouth
into which the world is disappearing.

from
Idyllen und Illusionen.
Tagebuchgedichte (1989)

On one of these quiescent days I read
of a giant that sacrificed himself, becoming
that which surrounds me: from his bones there grew
the mountain that rises there beyond the lake
(his eye) and is reflected in the water,
his blood. His black hair turned into
forests, his memory is flying,
a bird, up in the evening sky,
casting a shadow on the earth below,
his face, itself concealed behind a mask –
his knowledge – which keeps in careful check his laughter.

I went down to the lake and dipped my hand
into the cold blood, climbed then over bones,
that crunched like clinker, up towards the summit
and, through the camouflage of shaggy hair,
I gazed into the darkness of his eye
which fish had set twitching. A wind arose,
lifting the weary corners of his mask,
and freeing peals and peals of clear, bright laughter
which put all birds to flight, emptied the sky.
What's here is no-man's-land, the law of which –
unwritten – is to have to wait... and wait.

You see the strenuous labour of destruction,
the downfall of the species, you see fragments.
Where others glorify form, you say: there's nothing
but shards. Your book of books: the dictionary
of Power. In slanting letters on your door,
the words: this is a house of cards. Whoever
enters gets buried. When I put my trust
in permanence, you see too well the tremor
beneath my eye. Time to take stock? There isn't;
folly alone can still make a fool of history.
You see me as I'd like to see myself.

At issue is *this* rivulet, *this* snail –
the beggarly way it moves from stone to stone.
At issue: words; the surface of a hand
holding the mystery. Also fairy-tales –
the fool, his goblet (all his drams are dreams).
At issue: things in which we must believe,
which testify to our mortality.
At issue: Beauty, Power, Disgrace.
And what's without memory: its arduous path
does not fill the snail with *doubt*, the rivulet
renews itself while flowing: all *trompe l'oeil*.

Happy times: the forests return;
and the rivulets ramble once more through the meadows,
singing again; and the dreams are growing, serene,
in the grass; the coal crackles brightly to bits in the fire.
Someone's dissecting animals to find out the causes
of mental derangement, dejection, depression;
someone else, sweat beading his brow,
is studying God's inveterate ruses.
And yet another is asking on what
the stones in the rich soil live and is sharing
their half-asleep anguish under the sun.

As proof that he had existed there once,
he buried a whetstone under the wooden
threshold; set out. He saw the world, the blood
of the sun spurting vertically up into heaven, saw
the way a drop fell and killed the earth.
He also heard the mutters of dread as wolves drew near,
and also the cosmos' grinding grating. Matter
distended. Having outgrown his father's teachings,
he made his way back, and there at his side was a speckled pig.
The house, as was usual then, was a ruin. The whetstone alone
bore witness that he had existed there once.

Here on the edge of the forest, beneath the mendicant maple,
the boards for the dead, already half buried.
Wild cherries are casting a shadow
which keeps the brief path cool
between Herod's house and the house of the priest,
and raspberry, elder and dog-rose
make the transition more easy.
Beetles are giving cryptical details
on how far wood has merged with earth.
Someone who wished to join order and chaos
is sticking out of the ground here, head-down.

Alexandria missed, Sicily never arrived in,
Cheapside bypassed where the money-broker's child
was born. There are candles at every window,
shepherd's purse in acid meadows, and fumes
staining the aprons, the spotted waistless jackets.
Rifts in ground that is parched with too much history,
with philosophical filth. And repeatedly someone
who does not trim his mighty thousand-tongued beard
to the wind, who does not bemoan
the shortness of life, the unenlightened
state of things, as silly fools do.

You've lost your way in fairy-tales. Your only escort:
crossbills that tried (in vain) to extract
the nails from the hands of the Lord. You pass
uninhabited villages by where ramblers
darken the door-jambs and lintels, where moss
has crawled its way over the roofs, carpet-thick.
Saints are sitting wearily on spotted clouds,
counting Poverty, Meekness, Charity
on their fingers, loaded down with privileges.
Skulls grow out of the loessial soil,
look at you, melt back into the mist.

No soul for miles around; the washing
is loudly reeling about on the line, and fungi are drying
away on the insides of weathered window cavities.
On the church – with its incompatible towers –
the crumbling doves are being fed seed,
al fresco, by some wrinkled fingers.
There on the corner, bleached: the black rat
from childhood, turned almost white by the dust
that is rising like smoke. I start, as though
I'd been under a spell, an evil spell,
and see the dove, a rusty nail held fast in its beak.

Winter closed over the land amidst the applause
of the sedge. Brownish ochre was brightly
lining the loamy bank, my heart
a watery sponge. The birds had taken to flying
underwater, invisible animals
dug communications trenches under the snow.
Foam on the stones, pulled to bits by the north wind.
Every winter they pile a heap of stones
on the body, putting cranberries
on the top for the animals. Somewhere a fire
and the feeling that Time is cracking, shattering, in the flames.

Behind the shed, where a scrawny lawn
covers the static scree, there has been growing,
since the snow melted and the ground –
a mix of loam and clay and sand and gravel –
appeared again, a plant never found
in these parts before. The postman too, who has
no interest in letters but knows his botany,
stares in disbelief at the hirsute stem,
shaggy and full of glands, at the capitate stigma;
he runs his fingers across a yellowy bulge
and says, as he hands me the bills, 'expelled by culture'.

And higher up now, closer to the sun,
he shows me plants with stiff hair on their leaves,
fine-veined, whose corollas, near the bottom,
are peppered with purple glands. 'Only in Braunau,'
he says, 'up to now', and the baa-baa of the lambs,
obliviously cropping the rarity, appears
to be agreement. 'Plants are travelling faster,
chemistry's giving them wings; just look at these
three tips on the corolla's lower lips.
Obstinate Bag, Obese Big-Mouth,'
he says, and is gone with his mail-bag.

Snow on the fields and ice in the furrows;
the order revealed makes us look on the
white side: if what is hidden grows visible,
we're destined to perish; and, if it does not,
we can't put our trust in life. You yourself,
with your wealth of illusions, are nothing, nothing;
a thousand paths lead to the kingdom
of common sense, like damp,
or theft, or murder, or loss of one's papers,
and whatnot. Empty, you'll reach the centre;
empty, you'll leave it again, and white.

Death genuflects *and Light is out to win* –
an easy triumph after this long winter.
The sun's first rays turn pages pale, efface
the script; the ciphers flee into the books'
interior. A light breeze, leafing through,
exposes what each page was harbouring:
a bevy of grimaces, acid remorse,
and one iota of future, vain conceits
that flowed from the pen in the winter. Lovely prose –
also a vague pain eating its way outwards.
The light is going out now, Death will win.

When the water's confined in ice,
the surface pitted with little dimples,
animals, winter hair shaggy and long,
flit over the lake. All moving things
are seeking appropriate asylum. The track
of a hare, a hieroglyph in the snow, and – nearer
the shore – a herd of roe deer, and behind that
a dismal cluster of houses. The light
at the windows can't scare, can't keep away Night.
Everything happens at once, disappears –
as you do too with your daft melancholy.

There is a time for everything.
Thus ours has come: without voice, without echo.
Vainly, the questioning eye scans the slopes,
the snow, the coat, the hands that are dangling –
alien, cumbersome – out of the sleeves. There down beneath us:
wide, deep lakes and porphyry cliffs and also granite,
bottomless bogs in the valley. And from the village: clatter;
you cannot, however, trust your ears
(your ears feel like pasteboard!). Finally stars:
they'll never accompany Man again
and yet they warmly light his way astray.

Again the ownerless dog runs by,
like every evening, his fur full of burrs.
He must stray around all day in the copse,
alarming the other creatures. One ear
is in rags, one eye blind – it's not exactly
a pretty sight. He sometimes comes
through the hole in the fence and cocks his head
on one side and looks up barmily.
I tell him bittersweet nothings he seems
to like to hear. He only makes off
when I get up to go and fetch him some food.

Today he stays, his shaggy head
on his paws, and blinks askance at the sun
that's setting, too red. He sighs
so heavily when I ask him where he's from that dust
whirls up; but that is all. Hungry? I ask.
He's worn-out, crabbed. Are you fed up
with life, I ask, fed up with lice?
With roads, with squares, with sundown after sundown?
Sated with sights and smells? He looks at me,
dubiously, no, pitilessly, gets
trembling to his feet, slopes off.

I stay put, staring after him.
What is your name, I ask the gathering night:
you must have, sometime, answered to some name –
Hector or Anthony, Dog, Odysseus, Bonzo?
May you – lame dog – be called Odysseus.
Then you will surely have a few adventures,
will soon get home, will sort the suitors out,
will never age, will never limp again.
You'll tell them all what happened in the woods,
and won't forget to tell them of the man
who once, one evening, gave you a name.

The bungling gardener, who's got his cards,
is feeding the birds which are hopping with wonder,
is scattering seeds on the pebbles: nothing goes to waste.
Or everything. Just think of curative poisons, of ashes.
Invincible: so the forms seemed that splinter
underfoot. The bungling gardener,
without instructions, is sweeping up scraps, is
putting up chairs: he's waiting for us, his shady friends.
We, in our jolly shabbiness, though, send the child on ahead;
it is trembling all over. They're at the table together now,
and the garden's suffused with a right royal warmth.

Coolness rounds up the swallows, the pigeons
are all ruffled up beneath the eaves. You know what it means:
to want to salvage what cannot be salvaged –
the shadow you cast; the virgin light
when roofs start to colour; the mendicant eye
in front of paintings; the tenuous ends of experience;
also defeats and motley lies; the still
uncut grass; the obituary note on
Rage. Two days, or years, eternities:
nothing suffices. Not even Love any more, in the grip
of bureaucrats who, brazen-faced, file it.

Are things as they were? Does the ground
still crunch underfoot as it did
once? And have you got round
to reading the diary of grass,
each letter saluting. The door –
. the same vain creak as before –
gives too quickly, one darkens
the hall too lightly, opens
the windows: the water is changing
colour, the moon on the wane.
We go in the other direction.

Nothing but dreams! Still so far from the goal
of all we once hoped for. A verdant carpet
of moss, undulating countryside: the giants
of Nature are waking up for the final trial.
Day breaks slowly above the vast gulf
of the vanishing world, and the ice-church
rises beneath the barren, spindly moon.
A high, plaintive sound, then a grumbling,
rumbling, followed by silence. Reason is born
when the blind fight the blind: it's just as simple
as blinking or winking, as playing with signs.

Into the rain, the scales washed away from one's
eyes. Leave the cat, leave knowledge, leave books behind,
incarcerated in memory, dust. A coin
on the road, heads or tails, wet leaves, no, nothing
to hold you back: timeless, untouchable, soiled,
you're attractive to Chance. The department store first,
then theatre, opera, abattoir, clinic.
Brought up to be happy, to know how to open
the eyes of beautiful Grief, of the twilight
between two lines. And nature? A rock of grace
embraced by coarse roots, exposed in the rain.

Set out for home, forego Happiness;
Sorrow is being sized up: she alone,
who once ran away from Hope, can now guide us.
Things are remarkable, not the sangfroid
of permanence, time. From the clinic: music,
parting the rain; we set foot, dry, on the
other side. To touch life? A life that's a match,
a real match, for the transformed forms?
In China, in cloudy weather, they told
the time from the pupils of cats. All that counts
are things that everyone knows: opportunity makes the artist.

Deep in the forest a church, lived in
by spiders and wood-lice. In the apse's
ruins swallows, their boisterous cheeping
sounds out of tune, even more out of tune than
the echo. The driving force: vacuity.
Ants in the side-altar, clearing away,
in minute fragments, the cross, hardworking
iconoclasts. Dirt on the windows,
rattling frames in the wind, a shadow
sweeps across the cracks in the floor: it was not
summer cloudlets that cast a shadow like that.

A storm is approaching, and raindrops are dribbling
through the windows. One speaks, if at all,
of ultimate things with the visor of irony
firmly down. Charity, Justice –
absence makes the mind grow famished. *Our
goal, our repose and the end of discord*:
practising, exercising Freedom.
Our Yes sounds embarrassed, as does the No
that we owe to our morals. White flashes outside
and thunderclaps; we'd stop at nothing,
not even at swearing we're only dreaming.

As though at the flick of a switch, the sun –
suddenly – over the dug-up earth. One god
is dogging the other into the steaming light.
Who's leading, who's lagging? No more journeys
to find the Old in the Old. Thrust your hands
into your pockets and lift up your eyes
to the crowns of the beeches. Nail yourself
to the spot, without 'ahs', without 'ohs' –
no emotion. There in the distance: queues of cars,
characters pressed down into the fields.
And none of us opens his or her mouth.

Like an idea that remains invisible
on the various screens, not to be grasped
nor effaced, you run through history,
changing your views before they change
you, changing your coat and your shoes.
In the window your postcards turn yellow;
Kind Regards can be read, from outside,
from the birds' perspective. I make do
with volcanoes, old views of cities,
weathering slowly until the postman
brings new ones the rain has defaced.

Books with uncut pages, fanaticisms,
which only beetles read and silverfish,
like quiet commas between the grand abstractions:
Good and Evil; Beautiful, Ugly; Useful,
Harmful, the whole long litany of the imitation
of God. And the hand which does the cutting: friend
and enemy, both assailant and assailed.
And that which has no name? Receives a name:
the Other, Alien, Man-Without-Names
who squats there speechless on the ground and
writes with a finger on the dust.

Tempests, head winds. The mighty ocean winced only
once in its sleep and already we find ourselves
beached. Are interpreting traces: hands, dragging feet
in the yielding sand, and traces of men
and of beasts. And images up on the cliffs –
men with high foreheads, devoid of all trace
of pity for those who've arrived too late
who now are resting, in silence (that's fitting),
in some little nook that's already been bagged.
A dewdrop has formed in the course of the morning;
now it is falling, gets quenched in the sand.

A happy man, a sign-setter by trade,
guided by gods whom he saw at work
everywhere: on the threshold, in books,
even between the lines of the paper.
Not possessed because unsystematic
(systems were playthings). No Studies in Honour
of this latecomer. Only in dreams,
that pursued him like faithful dogs, did he see
the machinations of fate: trip-
wires between the signs, making him
fall. And never a safety-net when he awoke.

151

The book is broken-backed, its pages foxed;
there is a certain whiff of finishing school.
The birds that nest there in its innards
are pecking sentences into a pile
to print, or for the rubbish-heap, who knows.
A feverish hallucination penned
in Latin ink – alas Protagoras,
your doubt has cost you dear. At first a mere
stomach upset, then suddenly the fish
were speckling you, blood-red around the mouth
and spotted as though with incandescent sparks.

Stored on no chip. He found himself late,
if at all. And got on with himself
poorly. Patient gazes down at his
pencil: 'My weapon against old age
and...' No files, no RAMs, no ROMs,
no house. Just long, fixed looks through alien windows
at tables where paper was curling up
to protect its words. No allegories;
instead a bleak theatrum mundi, bridges
and ice. At times, in dreams, heroic
rhythms. And, in his trouser-pockets, stones.

Harsh is the toil of forgetting, harsh
and baseless. Childhood, Part One of the
harlequinade, reappears, unrevised.
It smells of printer's ink and of cellars.
Verses emerge with internal rhymes. Ships
languidly glide across the water, then sink.
Withdrawal of all one's moments, the brain unhoused,
out of its depth where there is no sea-
floor. In this ocean of universal signs
you will founder. Was that what you really wanted?
Come, I shall make the gap in my memory my haven.

Back to the stones, to gentle violence,
back to the seasons, *societies without power:*
it's just an incongruous fiction.
The candle is burning down, going out. He had
one great goal in life: a state-
funeral, nothing less, all the guests
in the rain. *Fame too demeans,*
the priest would have to say, and then,
like Job, on his bier, down into the grave,
and the drenched guests would nobly have to intone
the lofty chorale of meaning and being.

The wind hunts for food in the grass,
passes on; and rain, dampness, leaves
are calling you; and heretical weeds
are bowing their deeply uneasy heads.
Above the yapping and yelping of dogs,
on tenterhooks, Truth – the enemies
lick up the dust. And the tears,
in which Hatred flows, are long since
dry. Nothing impels you
to settle, seek honour:
exultant, you send the people away.

The last ray of light struck 'self-assessment',
then: utter darkness. Just the chalk face
on the wall opposite, its bright smile,
gleamed: don't contradict for there's nothing at stake.
We give back everything that we don't need;
the letters end up in the secret archives
in which devoted souls are collecting: manner and style,
legal incapacity, terror. Some of God's creatures,
more than engrossed, count up what counts:
in a low voice, they name the child
that's giving the chalk face a different name.

Dignity ages, the casing of
the worlds wears out, grown thin the fabric
of Love. 'Removed – address unknown'
adorns letters that jostle
for space with bank statements. Problems?
Rarely. A righteous fellow,
grown old in love, is what the books say.
Then he fell from the realms of transcendence
on to the pavement, a blatant case
for the local Red Cross. As to his writings:
stuff to make wreaths from.

And who is the father and king
of all things? The wry-mouthed guy
in the cowboy-boots who starts the
life-and-death quarrel by shooting,
out to put a joke end to
the world? Or the spasmodic flashing
there on the screen, all medium, no message?
What is it we keep falling out about,
you and me and all the rest?
One man, raving, raises his hands and spits
in the fire. Another tells Peace to get stuffed.

Religion, Culture – little coins
in dusty old jugs, still good for barter,
but not for commerce. The end of mourning,
illumination: a wind from the country
inclines us to hope, but brings with it fever.
Once more the whimpering, beefing breaks out;
collectors go round; the prices go up;
the unpaid invoice has got to be settled.
Why all the panic, the great big fuss?
Were people really expecting Apocalypse Sometime, expecting
a fall in admission-prices? No way.

Worry about the world? You've no memory!
Flowers, shamefaced, incline their heads
whenever we lie in the grass and survey
the sun – yesterday, and again and again.
Describing one day is describing them all
if you're looking heavenwards,
cultures beneath you, the jumble of altars,
cathedrals, worms and fungi. States
gnawed to bits by busy bacteria, marble,
along with remains of corpses. The sun
burns a hole in your will to celebrate life.

What did he say? I am tired of your
beauty. Tired of your language that turns
daily bane into bread and wine. Your tricks
leave me cold, your verities too,
just as perpetual as the north wind
which bears us the rumble of guns and songs
and the odour of newsprint.
The river is grey with the rust of your factories,
and soggy money is whirling, swirling about in the eddies.
Here I should build a house, a container
for all the letters that never reached you?

He dies – the eyes empty; the fullness of his teaching:
forgotten. A write-up in the paper:
unread. One language we speak:
we ought to all think and act as one.
Rubbish! Just look at this woman's hands,
at that man's ground-hugging gait, at the lines
on the children's brows, at the slight –
but apparently motiveless – trembling. The lie
of the land, and walls, and barbed-wire, and books,
just as always: except that, after his death, no one's left
who will keep his eyes skinned for mankind, for kind men.

A man in a visored cap is speaking:
for twenty years I've been living here;
history, baloney, pallid languishing
for a long life: for infinity.
I'd give an arm for you: I'm at home
in any darkness, no stone at all
could stop me striding onwards. Writing,
deep in the night, is a candle brightly
lighting a way for the self, for the secretly
darkening world. I'm glad we may age
on the shoulders of feeble giants, may die.

Hats off! The dance of the scapegoats seems
quite something in this lukewarm TV night.
The sceptic laughs; the frivolous
are glad Democracy does have
some sort of substance. Abortion, the East, the unemployed,
all taped – and peace just round the corner too.
Cockaigne! The only problem, sadly:
the penchant for brevity, the idée fixe
of total terseness means our seers' visions
might not be seen. But when the deluge comes,
no one will thirst. Till then: cut it, give over!

Race, newspaper. The Spirit of the Age
puffs out its cheeks with words and gobs at you:
Genetically speaking, the human species
will go downhill since those who have the most
offspring contribute the least to Progress.
Great Julian, suffer the positive children
to come to you so as not to perish,
gaoled in the footnotes of your science.
Stalin's genes, not bad. And the genes
of the woman across the street who is heaving
her heavy belly out of a room, into the sun?

The walls need whitewashing, cracks and stains
are appearing, decay. What exactly determines
on what terms a proposition is true?
Watery daybreak, ashes of light,
Truth keeps rapidly changing its signs.
On crooked lines, crooked missives: the call
for muzzles; self-eclipse; and philosophers
busy disputing sense, which is Greek to them.
Richer and robbed – creation of metaphors,
choice of masks: where language loses
its good reputation, strong words rule (o.k.).

In panic, the nymph bursts into the park
and searches for her plinth in the moonlight,
startling lovers who gird up their loins.
Sublime motifs? The Alps and stones –
scrap soaked in moonlight, a species of yellow
the coarse brush drips in ponderous drops.
Audibly, footsteps crunch on the gravel-path
petering out beyond a summerhouse
in between firs, a sombre Styx that
animals leap across in terror. Off with Beauty
to the museum – pack it off smartly, the beautiful world.

Unneedful, the play of the clouds, deceitful
the great big tears they have cribbed from third-rate
theatricals, making the mirrors mist over.
Nothing but bustle and empty pretence.
A genuine tragedy for the living,
and even the drowning, far out at sea,
would wish for a somewhat brighter exit.
Still, the painters rush to their easels;
'Ashes of Light' is the name of their theme.
Such a feast of dark when the clouds,
drab and cantankerous, strut their brief hour.

A land of reproach, a land of ill humour,
a land running out of experience,
thinking in images of a land
where slow fires burn the stalks of potatoes, where
children have gaping knees and sing: of a
land where grey and white lies steal past
on cat's paws, and where a king holds sway
in a land whose name is Intent:
but the king is asleep in the train
and only awakes at the terminus,
at the border, and this is in flames.

Sometimes you fit into one single sentence,
sometimes you're just too much for a book;
telegrams put you most pointedly,
travelling words cicatrized
by a ticker. Every pencil
will, one day, breathe its last, all ink
will, one day, run dry; and then you'll be left,
forlorn, at your desk, will praise
the world that's outside your window,
also the ancient stationer's shops
where Life stayed unscathed.

Stabbing neuralgia; too much language
where speech should have decently yielded to silence.
Card-catalogues chock-full, too, of gobbets:
Intention and mystery and competence,
bait for the head which courts emptiness,
entangled, entrapped, in self-realization.
And look after look after look: nothing seen;
and ash in the hands that were meant to protect
the fire; and they say that that which is bright
is only the cloak of that which is dark.
Alack, my headache, keep questioning.

A bird's eye view, but from higher
than birds can fly: the world
seems a slide, a specimen; 'things' and 'movement'
melt beneath the exalted eye, and freeze
when it reaches its zenith. Words too
pretend to be dead which, moments before,
were busy describing the teeming. A verse
from the universe taking in all that lies scattered
around in time: it would be a tombstone.
Look, thank heavens, dolphins, harbingers of storms;
semicolons that structure the surface.

He who tests the heat of the water
won't throw himself in: a classical maxim
devised when the world was the house of the strong,
run by weakness, by violent passions, by death.
Alas, faint-hearted century, two spots on your skin
and you're desperately scrambling to find your pen.
One's got to propose and dispose all oneself,
must not be ghost-written: that is self-love,
invulnerable, contant. And immortality,
our immortality: talkative, sad.
And please don't go thinking I'm only joking.

When climbing the stairs, take care to get into
the groove that's been worn by a thousand shoes.
When you enter the house, take hold of the
shiny doorknob grasped by a thousand hands.
Take the old cup, with its broken handle,
the dish with the crack. And look at those paintings
that no applause varnished, the rickety table.
When helped to wine, ask for water – in words
that in no way smack of eternity.
Of all birds, devote yourself to the sparrow,
then to the crow. Praise the grass, praise the lichen.

from
Hinter der Grenze (1990)

Chinoiserie

The books begin there at the end.
From the heights, the haunt of phoenixes, dragons,
the earth appears small:
the roofs decayed, the beams unsound,
the ponds overgrown.
When the wind rages and when the rain
falls unseasonably,
the people are restless.
A shadowless drawing in Chinese ink; stone upon stone.
A small boy has lain down flat on the ice
to get it to melt
and already the carp's thrashing round in the pot.
Lizards must realize Man's
desires: wealth, a long life, and quietude, virtue,
a dignified death. The dead take away the earth
from the living. One venerates trees,
the perpetual peach, the man who is
metamorphosed by learning. Make yourself older
than you are; old age is the rage here.
Those talking twaddle are healed with fox-meat.
If life is a closed book, how will you get
the measure of death? A cloud is parting
the landscape; a tree is getting bent back;
in front of it are a swollen-backed horse,
a camel, tigers, and dragons with skin like lustreless pearls.
Leave the door slightly ajar to allow
the spirit of the door to enter, and take off
neither hat nor belt – you'd offend your host.
Eat up your words and treat all paper
with due respect: protect it
from misuse. Drive the nail
into the wall further north and make your bed in the south.
The man who dies exits left, and right
the man who survives. White is, in China,
the colour of mourning.

From Romania, as it once was

I am the law, he said, the people's
cloak, and you lot: you are my tongue.
My wife wears a necklace
composed of fresh hearts, for only he
who opts for Beauty lives forever.
When I go riding, the crepitation
of sunflowers turning their heads to face me!
Only their roots waste away in the soil.
Faced with me, all wonders die down,
all oceans run dry.
Our heirloom: a narrative, our law;
everything else is merely the source of error and conflict.
Our peasants eat part of our happiness,
the rest wolfs itself.
When building our houses, we put
some milk in with the mortar.
Our poets lost their voice;
with a leathery finger they're circling
right around Yearning, never reach it.
My people does what a people should do:
it bows right down. The eagle, I say,
above the long lines of prostrate necks, is devouring corpses,
not the reptant mistletoe which is
frizzing our hearts, which is breaking our hearts.
A ruler was only allowed to reign
for thirty years, then the people destroyed him:
he who doctors the calendar dies –
such is the custom.

Far Beyond Prague

I
Did the Son of God feel ill
at ease among sinners? Our prayers strengthen
Him, not us, if they reach Him.
We live. We love the earth; our lives
are engrossed in the soil. We are the haulm:
once a year we get mown,
once thrashed. Nature here
has no interest at all in improving
Man. Through us God is strong;
His doctrine is simple, but hard to live up to.
Our poets still know the moon
above the plain; but of coal, of oceans
they're ignorant. Those who are too fond
of newfangled things are quick to forget, are impoverished.
We are the centre: the centre of Europe,
doting on oldfangled things.

II
Those who are too fond of oldfangled things
go to rack and ruin.
The wise man, you see, may not govern here:
he does not represent the people.
The people are just too small for the party.
Where *are* the people? the functionaries call
when they drive out on Sunday. As a result,
the party – as elsewhere in Europe – has ruled
that no expectations be placed in the people
so as to limit the disappointment. The meaning of new things
gets lost in form, but the party, its eye –
day and night – on our weal and woe, has no time
to search for it. Thus we are left
with form. We lose, hands up,
to our systems. They are simple,
too simple for men, and that is their strength.

165

III

Robbers used to infest these parts
who *made us pay tribute, a squirrel*
from every homestead. Today? We simply don't know
what we're still permitted to love. The Useful
is rarely good in these parts, the Beautiful
way out of reach of our funny money.
Our language: unknown beyond the
border. Only the summer sun, when it stands
in the south, can be understood, so poets say,
concrete infinitude all around them.
We mellow slowly, methodically. The law
of change and permanence was done away with
here by men. Depth, they say,
knows only one direction, too little. Here we live:
here on the outermost edge of attention,
here where the picture has long since been framed.
It's hardly a turn for the better that leaves
are falling from trees.

Near Budmerice

for Milan Richter

Evening hastily empties
the table piled high,
for the Advent, by the sun.
Lightless, the synagogue.
Late, the grubs fall
into autumn and die
when the weather turns foul.
God gives to the poor,
and helps the rich
live. The smell of coal,
of smoke. May a stone
be certainty: both preach
the same sermon.

Why is rain
an image of ruin?
Mushrooms, still sealed,
on the castle meadow
in Budmerice, seemingly forged.
Why do we feel no regret
when recalling the words
for mourning? Turn them over,
for everything's in them,
error too;
each handful is occupied –
conquest and play.

Above the mouse-grey woods,
a blurred moon.
Give up Man,
then the world will clear.
And the Lord will pray
while we're busy sleeping.

Skácel

The lateness of the hour
drove him home. Another drink,
a cigarette, a word
that will pass through the Jewish Gate
with its fluttering tongues.
*Once a year someone
hangs himself,* from someone
else's hand the world falls.
Neat little verses can't
outface Death, the Moravian
Master. Here in Brünn
the snow is like dust.
Your dark eyes
beneath their burning brows,
your shirt full of burrs.
Another week
and we'll see one another;
you've been dead six days.

Cahors

Someone who's come unannounced is standing
deep in the twilight: making
the silence grow
beneath the ploughed-up clouds.
We understand him,
understand his unreasonable joy.

As though beneath trees in the winter
when the final leaf,
only moments ago the world's mirror,
spins down, spins down,
strikes the ground.

Cathedrals like trees.
Hugging the trunk like a lover,
unasked, someone's
standing there and decoding the boughs.

20th October 1989

Outside my window, right before my eyes,
Orion's dog, white Sirius, is sniffing
away through the hungry branches, cool, bedewed,
suspended in infinite distance. Near things are blurred;
the radio's reedy voice: the capital
moves slowly east, into the neck of the world.
Dark horses as they are, the dreamers lose
the wager with themselves, and are relieved:
the thin ice crackles, breaks
above the words. One past, one path;
renunciation of all other paths.
And then the birds return, desires
huddle together as do clouds.
Day breaks in the room. Oblivious,
disgusted by the shop-soiled range of moods,
I try to think the whole thing through, and through:
the world appears, dismembered, in a poem.

The thirsting oceans in your hands,
stones worn away by the water, and the withered woods;
a fist which simply cannot be clenched.
Soldiers are crossing the life-line, the place
where the land of Hunger begins with its sorrowful villages,
its salty houses built on soil that is full of scars.
Underground rivers, the pounding sound that is made by the world.
Flocks of birds are escaping from this hand, are drawing
the yardstick of Beauty on water,
and on Oblivion, Death. A bad balance-sheet.
Come, flick your wrist and make the world fall out.

Memory . . .

Memory,
the fugitive brand
on your various letters,
a perfect replica of the world.
Too huge the spaces
we wrought for ourselves,
too slow our steps
to measure them.
As to the question
of what has been planned for us:
lost
in the post.

Nero piled lead on his chest...

Nero piled lead on his chest
in order to make his voice
stronger. Every word:
a scar burnt into
the dirty slate that is memory.
Others live on the interest
from silence; questions too
are a livelihood.
A nail avails
against nightly raving,
a nail that's been torn from a sepulcre.
Once I knew someone
who made insects crawl
across the empty page
of his notebook, and who –
in the tenuous shadow-script –
read his life to the end.

Pin your bliss…

Pin your bliss on what's attainable,
what's not will tear out your eye:
lyreless Orpheus, noseless Apollo,
fragments lead to the loss of one's sight.
How do scorpions kill themselves, do you know?
The Guanchos used to desiccate their dead
like halibut, like stockfish,
and put them, in pairs, in caves.
Nothing is lost. Ubiquitous hunger;
people poisoned to death by ambition.
How do scorpions kill themselves: you know.